GDANꙄꓘ

TRAVEL GUIDE

2024

Embracing the Baltic Beauty: A Comprehensive Exploration of Gdansk, Poland's Coastal Gem, in 2024"

Table of Contents: Gdansk Travel Guide 2024

Introduction

Local Transportation
Shopping in Gdansk

Chapter 11: Conclusion

INTRODUCTION

Welcome to the captivating city of Gdansk, where history, culture, and maritime charm come together to create a truly unique travel experience. Nestled on the Baltic Sea coast in northern Poland, Gdansk is a city with a rich and storied past, offering travelers a blend of medieval architecture, maritime heritage, and a vibrant modern spirit. As you embark on your journey through Gdansk in 2024, allow this travel guide to be your trusted companion, unveiling the secrets and treasures that await you in this splendid destination.

Gdansk, often referred to as the "Pearl of the Baltic," has earned its place as one of Europe's hidden gems, drawing travelers from around the world with its picturesque landscapes, historical significance, and warm hospitality. Whether you're a history enthusiast eager to explore the echoes of World War II, a culture lover ready to immerse yourself in the city's vibrant arts scene, a foodie seeking to savor Polish cuisine, or simply an explorer in search of new horizons, Gdansk has something to offer every type of traveler.

In this comprehensive Gdansk travel guide for 2024, we will embark on a captivating journey through the city's winding cobbled streets, delve into its fascinating history, and discover the modern delights that make Gdansk a dynamic and alluring destination. From the iconic landmarks of the Old Town to the lesser-known gems tucked away in the city's corners, we'll uncover the best that Gdansk has to offer.

So, as you prepare to set foot in this maritime marvel, let the pages of this guide be your compass, leading you to the heart of Gdansk's enchantment. Whether you're planning a short city break or a more extended stay, Gdansk promises a voyage of discovery, where every corner reveals a new facet of this splendid city's character. Get ready to be charmed by Gdansk's history, culture, and the warm embrace of its people as you embark on an unforgettable adventure in this coastal jewel of Poland.

What makes Gdansk a remarkable travel destination and what travelers can expect when exploring this enchanting city in 2024.

Historical Significance: Gdansk's history is a tapestry of stories, marked by periods of prosperity, conflict, and resilience. The city's strategic location on the Baltic Sea made it a hub for trade and culture, resulting in a rich maritime heritage. It's famously known as the place where World War II began with the bombardment of Westerplatte, and it played a pivotal role in the Solidarity Movement, which ultimately led to the fall of communism in Eastern Europe.

Old Town Charm: The heart of Gdansk lies within its captivating Old Town, a meticulously restored area that transports visitors back in time. With its colorful facades, cobblestone streets, and charming squares, it's a place where every corner reveals architectural gems, historical sites, and delightful cafes.

Historic Landmarks: Gdansk boasts an impressive array of historic landmarks, including St. Mary's Basilica, an architectural masterpiece; Long Market (Dlugi Targ), lined with exquisite townhouses; the Great Arsenal, a testament to the city's maritime heritage; Artus Court, once a meeting place for merchants; Neptune's Fountain, an iconic symbol of Gdansk; and the Golden Gate, an imposing entrance to the Old Town.

Museums and Cultural Attractions: Gdansk's cultural scene is thriving, with numerous museums and attractions to explore. The National Maritime Museum offers insights into the city's maritime history, while the Museum of the Second World War provides a comprehensive look at the war's impact. The European Solidarity Centre is a testament to the power of solidarity in the fight for freedom. The city also boasts cultural venues like the Shakespeare Theatre and the Gdansk Philharmonic Hall.

Culinary Delights: Polish cuisine takes center stage in Gdansk, offering a delightful blend of flavors. From hearty pierogi (dumplings) to aromatic barszcz (beetroot soup) and the iconic kielbasa (sausage), food enthusiasts will find a plethora of dishes to savor. Gdansk's restaurants and street food stalls serve up local specialties that are sure to please every palate.

Vibrant Nightlife: As the sun sets, Gdansk comes alive with a vibrant nightlife scene. Explore nightclubs and bars where you can dance the night away or unwind with a cocktail. Live music venues offer a taste of local talent, and nighttime strolls along the city's illuminated streets are a charming way to cap off your day.

Day Trips and Outdoor Adventures: Gdansk serves as a gateway to numerous day trip destinations. Explore the medieval grandeur of Malbork Castle, the hometown of Copernicus in Frombork, or relax on the pristine beaches of the Hel Peninsula. Outdoor enthusiasts can venture into the Kashubian Switzerland for hiking and nature exploration.

Practical Information: The guide provides essential practical information, including details on currency and banking, communication and SIM cards, internet and Wi-Fi availability, medical services, local transportation, shopping, safety tips, and emergency contacts, ensuring a smooth and informed travel experience.

Gdansk in 2024 promises to be a captivating journey through time, culture, and maritime charm. Whether you're a history buff, a culture lover, a food enthusiast, or someone seeking unforgettable experiences, Gdansk offers a treasure trove of discoveries waiting to be explored. So, as you prepare for your visit, let this travel guide be your compass to unlock the wonders of this splendid coastal city in Poland.

1

Gdansk at a Glance

Nestled on the picturesque Baltic Sea coast in northern Poland, Gdansk is a city that effortlessly combines a rich history with modern vitality. Here's a snapshot of Gdansk's key highlights:

Historical Significance: Gdansk's history is marked by its role as a major Hanseatic

League trading port, making it a hub of commerce, culture, and maritime influence. It's also a city of historical milestones, from the outbreak of World War II at Westerplatte to the birthplace of the Solidarity Movement that led to the fall of communism.

Old Town Charm: The heart of Gdansk beats within its beautifully preserved Old Town, characterized by cobbled streets, colorful facades, and an abundance of historical architecture. It's a place where every corner reveals architectural gems, quaint cafes, and vibrant markets.

Historic Landmarks: St. Mary's Basilica, a towering Gothic masterpiece; Long Market (Dlugi Targ), lined with elegant townhouses; the Great Arsenal, a testament to Gdansk's maritime heritage; Artus Court, once a meeting place for merchants; Neptune's Fountain, an iconic symbol of the city; and the imposing Golden Gate are just a few of the historic landmarks that await exploration.

Museums and Culture: Gdansk is home to an array of museums, including the National Maritime Museum, Museum of the Second World War, and European Solidarity Centre, each offering a unique perspective on the city's history and culture. The city's cultural scene thrives with theaters, galleries, and music venues.

Culinary Delights: Polish cuisine takes center stage in Gdansk, with dishes like pierogi, barszcz, and kielbasa being local favorites. Restaurants, street food stalls, and markets provide ample opportunities to savor these culinary delights.

Vibrant Nightlife: As night falls, Gdansk comes alive with a vibrant nightlife scene. From trendy nightclubs to cozy bars and live music venues, there's no shortage of options for those seeking evening entertainment.

Day Trips and Outdoor Adventures: Gdansk serves as a gateway to exciting day trip destinations. Explore the medieval grandeur of Malbork Castle, the hometown of Copernicus in Frombork, or unwind on the beaches of the Hel Peninsula. Outdoor enthusiasts can venture into the Kashubian Switzerland for hiking and nature exploration.

Practical Information: This travel guide provides essential practical information to ensure a smooth visit, including details on currency and banking, communication options, internet accessibility, medical services, transportation, shopping, safety tips, and emergency contacts.

Gdansk's unique blend of history, culture, and coastal charm makes it a destination that appeals to a wide range of travelers.

Whether you're captivated by its historical significance, eager to explore its cultural offerings, or simply seeking to savor its culinary delights, Gdansk invites you to discover its treasures in 2024.

Gdansk's Historical Significance

Gdansk, often referred to as "Danzig" in historical contexts, holds a place of immense significance in European history. Its story is a testament to resilience, change, and the enduring spirit of its people. Here's a closer look at the historical importance of Gdansk:

Hanseatic Trading Power: In the Middle Ages, Gdansk was a vital member of the Hanseatic League, a powerful confederation of merchant guilds and market towns. Its strategic location on the Baltic Sea made it a central hub for trade between Western Europe, Scandinavia, and Eastern Europe. The city's prosperity during this period is evident in its stunning medieval architecture and grand merchant houses, which still stand in the Old Town.

Outbreak of World War II: Gdansk gained worldwide recognition as the site where World War II began. On September 1, 1939, the German battleship Schleswig-Holstein bombarded the Polish military post at Westerplatte, located in Gdansk's harbor. This event marked the start of the war and is a poignant reminder of the city's role in one of the most significant conflicts in history.

Solidarity Movement: Gdansk played a pivotal role in the struggle for democracy and workers' rights in the 20th century. The Gdansk Shipyard was the epicenter of the Solidarity Movement, led by Lech Walesa, which advocated for workers' rights and ultimately contributed to the fall of communism in Poland and across Eastern Europe. The European Solidarity Centre in Gdansk is a testament to this historic movement.

The Rebirth of a Nation: Gdansk's historical journey mirrors Poland's own path to independence and self-determination. The city's resilience in the face of wars, partitions, and occupation is a symbol of Poland's enduring spirit. Today, Gdansk stands as a thriving, vibrant city, proudly embracing its history while looking toward a bright future.

Cultural Heritage: Gdansk's historical significance is not confined to politics and warfare. It's also a city steeped in cultural heritage. Figures like the philosopher Arthur Schopenhauer and the astronomer Johannes Hevelius have left their mark on the city's intellectual and scientific legacy. Gdansk's cultural institutions, including theaters, museums, and galleries, continue to celebrate its rich history and artistic contributions.

Gdansk's historical significance is not just a chapter in the past; it's a living narrative that shapes the city's identity today. Visitors to Gdansk can explore this captivating history through its well-preserved architecture, museums, and cultural landmarks, gaining a deeper appreciation for the city's enduring spirit and the pivotal role it has played in Europe's story.

Geography and Climate

Gdansk's geographical location and climate play a significant role in shaping the city's character and appeal to travelers. Here's a closer look at the geography and climate of Gdansk:

Geographical Location:

Gdansk is situated in northern Poland, on the country's Baltic Sea coast. It lies at the mouth of the Vistula River, which is one of Europe's major rivers, flowing through several countries before reaching the Baltic Sea.

The city is part of the Pomeranian Voivodeship (province) and is the capital of the Pomeranian region.

Gdansk forms a metropolitan area with the neighboring cities of Sopot and Gdynia, collectively known as the "Tricity" (Trójmiasto in Polish). These cities are interconnected and provide a wealth of

cultural, recreational, and economic opportunities.
Coastal Beauty:

Gdansk's coastal location grants it access to the stunning Baltic Sea shoreline. The city's waterfront areas, including Brzezno Beach and Sobieszewo Island, offer beautiful sandy beaches and opportunities for seaside relaxation.
The Baltic Sea also contributes to Gdansk's maritime heritage, with a bustling port and a rich history of seafaring.

Climate:

Gdansk experiences a temperate maritime climate, characterized by relatively mild summers and cool winters.

The city's proximity to the Baltic Sea moderates its climate, leading to less temperature extremes compared to inland areas.

Summers (June to August) in Gdansk are generally pleasant, with average high temperatures ranging from 20°C to 23°C (68°F to 73°F). This is an ideal time for outdoor exploration and beach activities.

Winters (December to February) are cooler, with average highs around 2°C to 3°C (36°F to 37°F). Snowfall is common during this season, creating a picturesque winter atmosphere.

Spring (March to May) and autumn (September to November) are transitional seasons with mild temperatures, making them suitable for city sightseeing.

Rainfall: Gdansk receives a moderate amount of rainfall throughout the year, with slightly wetter conditions in summer and autumn. Visitors can expect occasional rain showers, so it's advisable to carry an umbrella or raincoat, especially during these seasons.

Baltic Sea Influence: The presence of the Baltic Sea not only moderates the climate but also contributes to Gdansk's maritime charm. Seafood is a prominent feature of the local cuisine, and the waterfront areas provide opportunities for water sports, boating, and enjoying scenic views of the sea.

Gdansk's geographical location on the Baltic coast, combined with its temperate maritime climate, makes it an appealing destination for travelers who appreciate a mix of historical exploration and coastal relaxation. Whether you're strolling through the Old Town's cobbled streets in the summer or enjoying the snowy enchantment of winter, Gdansk's climate and geography offer unique experiences year-round.

Travel Essentials for Your Gdansk Adventure

As you prepare for your journey to Gdansk in 2024, it's important to ensure you have all the necessary travel essentials to make your trip comfortable and enjoyable. Here's a list of travel essentials to consider:

Travel Documents:

Passport: Ensure it's valid for at least six months beyond your planned departure date.
Visa: Check the visa requirements for Poland based on your nationality and the purpose of your visit.
Travel Insurance: Purchase comprehensive travel insurance that covers medical emergencies, trip cancellations, and other unforeseen events.

Money and Banking:

Currency: The currency in Poland is the Polish Zloty (PLN). It's advisable to carry some local currency for small expenses.

Credit/Debit Cards: Notify your bank of your travel plans to avoid any issues with card usage abroad. Credit cards are widely accepted in Gdansk.

Communication:

Mobile Phone: Check with your mobile provider about international roaming options or consider purchasing a local SIM card in Gdansk for data and local calls.

Language: While Polish is the official language, English is commonly spoken in tourist areas. Having a basic Polish phrasebook can be helpful for communication.

Travel Adapters: Poland uses the European-style Type C and Type E electrical outlets. Bring the appropriate travel adapter to charge your devices.

Weather-Appropriate Clothing:

Check the weather forecast for Gdansk during your visit and pack clothing accordingly. Summers are generally mild, while winters can be cold.

Comfortable walking shoes are essential for exploring the city's cobbled streets.

Medications and Health:

Prescription Medications: Bring an ample supply of any prescription medications you may need during your trip.

First-Aid Kit: Include basic medical supplies such as adhesive bandages, pain relievers, and any personal essentials.

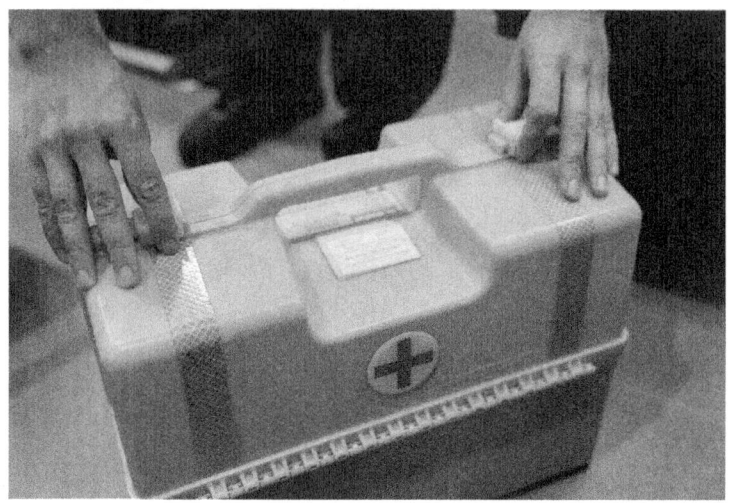

Travel Guides and Maps:

Carry a printed or digital copy of your Gdansk travel guide, city maps, and any relevant tourist brochures.
Download offline maps and travel apps to your smartphone for easy navigation.
Travel Backpack or Daypack: A small, lightweight backpack is useful for carrying

essentials during day trips and exploring the city.

Travel Locks: Ensure the security of your belongings by using luggage locks for your bags and hotel room doors.

Travel Insurance Documents: Carry copies of your travel insurance policy, emergency contact information, and any relevant medical records.

Travel Tickets and Itinerary: Keep your flight, train, or bus tickets, as well as your accommodation reservations, organized and easily accessible.

Reusable Water Bottle: Stay hydrated while reducing plastic waste by carrying a reusable water bottle.

Camera and Electronics:

If you're bringing a camera, remember extra memory cards, batteries, and chargers.
Power Bank: Carry a portable power bank to keep your devices charged while on the go.
Adapters for Gadgets: Bring any necessary adapters and chargers for your electronic devices.

Travel Toiletries:

Pack travel-sized toiletries in a clear, resealable bag to comply with airport security regulations.

Don't forget essentials like toothbrush, toothpaste, and personal hygiene items.
Entertainment: Consider bringing a book, e-reader, or other forms of entertainment for downtime during your trip.

Local Currency: Have some Polish Zloty (PLN) on hand for small purchases, transportation, and places that may not accept cards.

Travel Pillow and Eye Mask: These can enhance your comfort during long flights or train journeys.

Remember that Gdansk is a safe and welcoming city for travelers, but it's always wise to take precautions with your belongings and stay aware of your surroundings. By packing these travel essentials and staying organized, you'll be well-prepared to make the most of your Gdansk adventure in 2024.

2

When to Visit Gdansk

Best Time to Visit Gdansk

Choosing the right time to visit Gdansk can greatly enhance your travel experience, as the city's climate and events vary throughout the year. Here's a breakdown of the seasons and what to expect during each, helping you decide when to plan your Gdansk adventure in 2024:

1. Spring (March to May):

Spring in Gdansk brings milder weather, with temperatures gradually warming up.

This season is ideal for city exploration and cultural activities as crowds are relatively smaller than in summer.

You can witness the city's gardens and parks coming to life with colorful blooms.

2. Summer (June to August):

Summer is the peak tourist season in Gdansk, thanks to the warm and pleasant weather.

This is the best time for beachgoers, as the Baltic Sea waters are at their warmest.

Expect crowded tourist attractions and higher accommodation prices, so it's advisable to book in advance.

Gdansk hosts numerous festivals and outdoor events during the summer months.

3. Autumn (September to November):

Early autumn in September is still pleasant, with warm temperatures and fewer crowds compared to summer.

September is a great time for outdoor activities and sightseeing.

As autumn progresses, temperatures begin to cool, making it more suitable for those who enjoy brisk weather and fall foliage.

4. Winter (December to February):

Winter in Gdansk is cold, with temperatures often hovering around freezing or below.

This season is perfect for travelers who appreciate a winter wonderland and fewer tourists.

Gdansk's festive decorations and Christmas markets add a charming atmosphere during December.

Snowfall can create picturesque scenes, especially in January and February.

Special Considerations:

If you're interested in specific events or festivals, check the city's event calendar for dates that align with your interests. For example, St. Dominic's Fair in August is a major cultural event.

Keep in mind that Gdansk's coastal location means it can be a bit cooler and windier than inland areas, so pack accordingly, especially if visiting in spring or autumn.

Summary:

The best time to visit Gdansk depends on your preferences. Summer is perfect for beach lovers and festival-goers but comes with higher prices and crowds. Spring and early autumn offer milder weather and fewer tourists. Winter provides a unique and less crowded experience but requires preparation for cold conditions. Consider your interests and what kind of experience you seek when deciding on the best time for your Gdansk adventure in 2024.

Visa and Entry Requirements

Before embarking on your journey to Gdansk in 2024, it's essential to understand the visa and entry requirements for Poland, as they may vary depending on your nationality and the purpose of your visit. Here's an overview to help you plan your trip:

1. Visa Requirements:

European Union (EU) and European Economic Area (EEA) Citizens: If you are a citizen of an EU or EEA member state, you do not need a visa to enter Poland or any other Schengen Area country, including Gdansk. You can stay for an unlimited period as long as you have a valid ID or passport.
Non-EU/EEA Citizens: If you are a citizen of a country outside the EU/EEA, you may need a Schengen Visa to visit Gdansk. The

specific requirements and application process depend on your nationality and the purpose of your visit (tourism, business, study, etc.).

2. Schengen Area Membership:

Poland is part of the Schengen Area, which allows for passport-free travel between member countries. If you plan to visit other Schengen countries during your trip, your visa should be issued by the country where you intend to stay the longest or your initial entry point into the Schengen Area.

3. Visa Application Process:

Contact the Polish embassy or consulate in your home country or the relevant authorities responsible for visa issuance.

Start the visa application process well in advance of your planned travel dates, as it may take some time to process your application.

4. Required Documents:

Passport: Ensure your passport is valid for at least six months beyond your planned departure date.

Visa Application Form: Complete the visa application form provided by the Polish authorities.

Passport Photos: Provide recent passport-sized photos that meet the specified requirements.

Travel Itinerary: Present a detailed travel itinerary, including flight reservations, accommodation bookings, and an outline of your planned activities in Gdansk.

Travel Insurance: Purchase comprehensive travel insurance that covers medical emergencies and provides sufficient coverage for your entire stay.

Proof of Sufficient Funds: Show evidence of financial means to cover your expenses while in Gdansk, such as bank statements or a sponsorship letter if applicable.

Additional Requirements: Depending on your visa category (tourist, business, etc.), additional documents may be required.

5. Visa-Free Transit:

Some travelers may be eligible for visa-free transit through Poland if they are in transit to a non-Schengen destination and meet certain conditions. Check with your airline and the Polish authorities for specific transit visa requirements.

6. Customs and Entry Procedures:

Upon arrival in Gdansk, you will go through passport control. Ensure that your passport and visa (if required) are in order.

Be prepared to answer questions about the purpose of your visit and provide any requested documentation to border control authorities.

7. Visa Extensions:

If you wish to extend your stay in Poland while in Gdansk, you should apply for a visa extension at the local Voivodeship Office before your current visa expires.

It's essential to verify the most up-to-date visa requirements and procedures with the Polish embassy or consulate in your country or the official Polish government website. Ensure that you have all the necessary documents and visas before departing for Gdansk to avoid any entry issues and enjoy a smooth and memorable visit to this beautiful city in 2024.

Processes I took before my Gdansk travel Adventure

As I embarked on my Gdansk travel adventure in 2024, the excitement of exploring this historic city on Poland's Baltic Sea coast filled my heart. Little did I know that the journey would be just as enriching in the planning stages as it would be when I set foot in the charming streets of Gdansk.

Dreaming of Gdansk

I, a passionate traveler and history enthusiast, had long dreamt of visiting Gdansk. The city's rich history, maritime heritage, and picturesque Old Town had captured my imagination. One evening, as I scrolled through photos of Gdansk's colorful facades and the imposing Neptune's Fountain, I decided it was time to turn this dream into reality.

Research and Preparation

My journey began with extensive research. I delved into Gdansk's history, its cultural significance, and the best times to visit. I discovered that Gdansk's climate was temperate, with a peak tourist season in summer and a magical winter ambiance. Considering my preference for fewer crowds, I opted for a spring visit.

Visa Application

As I held a passport from a non-EU country, I knew I needed a Schengen Visa to enter Poland. Navigating the visa application process was a meticulous task. I gathered all the required documents, including my travel itinerary, insurance, and proof of financial means. The Polish embassy in my home country guided me through the steps, and after a nerve-wracking wait, I received the coveted visa.

Flight and Accommodation

With visa in hand, I eagerly booked my flights to Gdansk Lech Walesa Airport. It was a seamless process, and I opted for a convenient direct flight. Accommodation choices in Gdansk were diverse, from charming boutique hotels in the heart of the Old Town to modern waterfront options. I chose a cozy guesthouse near Long Market, ensuring easy access to Gdansk's historic treasures.

Packing and Anticipation

As the departure date approached, I meticulously packed my bags. Spring in Gdansk meant layering clothing for varying temperatures. I included my trusted walking shoes for exploring cobbled streets and a sturdy umbrella for any April showers.

Arrival in Gdansk

Stepping off the plane at Lech Walesa Airport, the crisp Baltic Sea air welcomed me to Gdansk. The immigration process was straightforward, and I presented my visa with confidence. Soon, I found myself in a taxi heading towards the Old Town, a place that had lived in my dreams for so long.

Gdansk Unveiled

My days in Gdansk were filled with awe and wonder. I roamed the narrow streets of the Old Town, admiring Gothic architecture, visiting St. Mary's Basilica, and enjoying pierogi in quaint cafes. The city's history came alive at the European Solidarity Centre, where the Solidarity Movement's story was told.

Unexpected Discoveries

One sunny afternoon, I ventured outside the city to Westerplatte, the site where World War II had begun. Standing amidst the remnants of history, I couldn't help but reflect on the significance of this place. Gdansk had an uncanny ability to intertwine the past with the present.

Farewell and Fond Memories

As my journey in Gdansk neared its end, I knew I had uncovered a treasure trove of memories. From savoring Baltic seafood to watching amber artisans at work, Gdansk had left an indelible mark on my heart.

Epilogue: A Journey of a Lifetime

My Gdansk travel adventure had been more than just a vacation; it was a journey through history and culture. It was a testament to the power of dreams and the magic of discovery. As I boarded the plane to return home, I knew that Gdansk would forever hold a special place in my traveler's soul, and I carried its stories with me, ready to inspire new adventures.

Budgeting for Your Gdansk Adventure

Embarking on a memorable adventure to Gdansk in 2024 is not only exciting but also requires careful budget planning. Here's a guide to help you create a budget that allows you to enjoy the best of Gdansk without breaking the bank:

1. Determine Your Overall Budget:

Start by determining the total amount you're willing to spend on your Gdansk adventure. This should include expenses for flights, accommodation, daily expenses, and activities.

2. Flights and Transportation:

Research flight options well in advance to find the best deals. Consider flying during off-peak times and using fare comparison websites.

Don't forget to budget for transportation to and from the airport.

Gdansk has an efficient public transportation system, so plan for bus or tram fares to get around the city.

3. Accommodation:

Choose accommodation that suits your budget and preferences. Gdansk offers a range of options, from budget hostels to luxury hotels.

Look for deals and promotions, especially if you book in advance.

Consider staying in the Old Town for a more immersive experience.

4. Daily Expenses:

Estimate daily expenses for meals, transportation within the city, and activities.
Gdansk offers a variety of dining options, including affordable street food and mid-range restaurants.
Plan for occasional dining at local eateries to savor traditional Polish cuisine without breaking the budget.
5. Activities and Sightseeing:

Research the attractions and activities you want to experience in Gdansk.
Look for combination tickets or city passes that offer discounts on multiple attractions.
Budget for entrance fees to museums, historical sites, and guided tours.
6. Currency Exchange and Banking:

Be aware of currency exchange rates and consider exchanging some currency in advance for convenience upon arrival.

Use ATMs in Gdansk to withdraw Polish Zloty (PLN) for daily expenses, as they offer competitive rates.

7. Contingency Fund:

Set aside a small contingency fund for unexpected expenses or emergencies.

8. Souvenirs and Shopping:

Allocate a budget for souvenirs and gifts. Gdansk is known for its amber jewelry and crafts.

Bargaining is not common in Poland, so be prepared to pay the marked prices.

9. Travel Insurance:

Include the cost of comprehensive travel insurance in your budget to cover unexpected events, such as medical emergencies or trip cancellations.

10. Tipping and Gratuity:

- While tipping is not obligatory in Poland, it's customary to leave a small tip for good service, typically rounding up the bill.

11. Miscellaneous Expenses:
- Plan for other potential expenses, such as SIM cards for data, airport transfers, and travel accessories.

12. Tracking Expenses:
- Keep track of your daily expenses using a travel budget app or a simple notebook to ensure you stay within your budget.

13. Flexibility:
- Allow some flexibility in your budget for spontaneous experiences or last-minute changes to your itinerary.

14. Finalize Your Budget:
- Once you've estimated expenses for each category, add them up to ensure they align with your overall budget.

By carefully planning your budget for your Gdansk adventure, you can enjoy this enchanting city to the fullest without worrying about financial stress. With a well-structured budget in place, you'll be ready to immerse yourself in the history, culture, and beauty that Gdansk has to offer in 2024.

Packing Tips and Essentials for Your Gdansk Adventure

Packing for your Gdansk adventure in 2024 requires a balance between practicality and preparedness. Here's a list of packing tips and essential items to ensure you're well-prepared for your journey:

1. Travel Documents:

Passport: Ensure it's valid for at least six months beyond your planned departure date.
Visa: If required, have your Schengen Visa or relevant travel permits.
2. Digital Copies:

Make digital copies of essential documents like your passport, visa, and travel insurance. Store them in a secure cloud storage service or email them to yourself for easy access in case of loss or theft.
3. Currency and Payment:

Polish Zloty (PLN): Bring some local currency for small expenses upon arrival.

Credit/Debit Cards: Notify your bank of your travel plans and carry cards for payments and ATM withdrawals. Credit cards are widely accepted.

4. Travel Adapters:

Poland uses European-style Type C and Type E electrical outlets. Bring the appropriate travel adapter to charge your devices.

5. Weather-Appropriate Clothing:

Check the weather forecast for Gdansk during your visit.

Spring (March to May): Layer clothing for varying temperatures, and pack a lightweight jacket or raincoat.

Summer (June to August): Pack lightweight and breathable clothing. Don't forget swimwear if you plan to visit the beach.

Autumn (September to November): Bring layers and a light jacket or sweater for cooler evenings.

Winter (December to February): Pack warm clothing, including a heavy coat, gloves, and a hat.

6. Comfortable Walking Shoes:

Gdansk's cobbled streets and historic sites require comfortable walking shoes or sneakers. Consider waterproof options for rainy days.

7. Umbrella and Rain Gear:

Gdansk experiences occasional rainfall, so bring a compact umbrella or a waterproof jacket with a hood.

8. Travel Backpack or Daypack:

A small backpack is handy for carrying essentials during day trips and exploring the city.

9. Travel Locks:

Use luggage locks to secure your bags and ensure the safety of your belongings.

10. Toiletries and Personal Care:

- Pack travel-sized toiletries in a clear, resealable bag for airport security.
- Don't forget essentials like toothbrush, toothpaste, shampoo, and any prescription medications.

11. Travel Towel and Laundry Supplies:

- A compact travel towel is useful for beach trips or as a backup.
- Consider packing a small amount of laundry detergent for hand washing clothing if needed.

12. Electronics:

- Camera and accessories if you're a photography enthusiast.
- Power bank for keeping your devices charged while on the go.
- Adapters and chargers for your gadgets.

13. Travel Pillow and Eye Mask:

- These can enhance your comfort during long flights or train journeys.

14. Entertainment:
- Bring a book, e-reader, or other forms of entertainment for downtime during your trip.

15. Water Bottle:
- Carry a reusable water bottle to stay hydrated and reduce plastic waste.

16. First-Aid Kit:
- Include basic medical supplies such as adhesive bandages, pain relievers, and any personal essentials.

17. Insect Repellent:
- Depending on the season and your activities, insect repellent can be useful.

18. Travel Apps:
- Download offline maps and travel apps to your smartphone for easy navigation and language translation.

19. Backpack Rain Cover:
- If you plan to hike or spend time outdoors, a rain cover for your backpack can protect your gear.

20. Travel Journal:
- Capture memories and jot down travel notes in a journal or digital note-taking app.

21. Snacks:
- Pack some snacks like granola bars or nuts for energy during excursions.

Remember to pack according to your personal needs and the specific activities you plan to enjoy in Gdansk. Keep your luggage organized, and don't overpack; leave some space for souvenirs and mementos from your unforgettable Gdansk adventure in 2024.

Language and Useful Phrases for Your Gdansk Adventure

While visiting Gdansk in 2024, you'll find that the official language is Polish. While many locals in tourist areas and younger generations may speak English, learning a few Polish phrases can enhance your experience and show your appreciation for the local culture. Here are some essential phrases and language tips to help you communicate effectively:

Basic Phrases:

Hello: Dzień dobry (jen DOH-bri) - Use this greeting during the daytime.
Good evening: Dobry wieczór (DOH-bri VYEH-choor) - Use this greeting in the evening.
Goodbye: Do widzenia (doh veed-ZEHN-yah)
Please: Proszę (PROH-sheh)

Thank you: Dziękuję (JEN-koo-yeh)

Yes: Tak (tahk)

No: Nie (nyeh)

Excuse me / I'm sorry: Przepraszam (psheh-PRAH-sham)

I don't understand: Nie rozumiem (nyeh roh-ZOO-myem)

Do you speak English?: Czy mówisz po angielsku? (chi MOH-vish poh ahn-GYEL-skoo)

Travel and Directions:

11. Where is...?: Gdzie jest...? (gdjeh yest)

Hotel: Hotel (hoh-TEL)

Restaurant: Restauracja (res-toh-RAH-tsya)

Train station: Dworzec kolejowy (DVOR-zets ko-LEH-yev-ee)

Bus station: Dworzec autobusowy (DVOR-zets ah-oo-to-BOO-soh-vi)

Airport: Lotnisko (LOHT-nee-skoh)

How much is this?: Ile to kosztuje? (ee-leh toh kohs-TOO-yeh)

Food and Dining:

18. Menu: Menu (MAY-noo)

Water: Woda (VOH-dah)
Breakfast: Śniadanie (SHNYAH-dahn-yeh)
Lunch: Obiad (oh-BYAHD)
Dinner: Kolacja (koh-LAHT-syah)
I would like...: Chciałbym/chciałabym...
(h-chyaw-BIM / h-chyaw-LAH-bim)
A table for two, please: Stolik dla dwóch
osób, proszę (STOH-lik dla DVUH-kh
oh-SOHB, PROH-sheh)
Shopping and Souvenirs:
25. How much does this cost?: Ile to
kosztuje? (ee-leh toh kohs-TOO-yeh)

I'm just looking: Tylko się rozglądam
(TYL-koh syeh roh-ZGWAH-dahm)
Can I pay with a card?: Czy mogę zapłacić
kartą? (chi MOH-geh zah-PLAH-chi
kar-TAH)
Emergencies:
28. Help: Pomoc (POH-mots)

I need a doctor: Potrzebuję lekarza
(poh-TSHEH-boo-yeh leh-KAHR-zah)

Police: Policja (poh-LEETS-yah)

I'm lost: Zgubiłem/zgubiłam się (zgoo-BEE-wem / zgoo-BEE-wahm syeh)

General Tips:

Learning a few basic phrases in Polish is appreciated by locals and can make your interactions more enjoyable.

Most signs in tourist areas are bilingual, with Polish and English.

Carry a small phrasebook or use translation apps to assist you in communication.

While English is widely understood, especially in tourist areas, making an effort to use some basic Polish phrases can enhance your experience and help you connect with the friendly people of Gdansk during your 2024 adventure.

Overview of Gdansk's Regions

Gdansk, a historic and vibrant city located on Poland's Baltic Sea coast, is divided into several distinct regions, each offering its own unique charm and attractions. Exploring these regions will allow you to discover the rich history, culture, and natural beauty of this captivating city. Here is an overview of Gdansk's main regions:

1. Old Town (Stare Miasto):

Gdansk's Old Town is the heart of the city and a testament to its historical significance. It features beautifully preserved medieval and Renaissance architecture, narrow cobblestone streets, and charming pastel-colored buildings.
Highlights: Neptune's Fountain, St. Mary's Basilica, Long Market (Długi Targ), and the historic Gdansk Crane (Żuraw).

2. Main City (Śródmieście):

Located just south of the Old Town, the Main City region is a bustling area with a mix of historic sites, modern amenities, and residential neighborhoods. It offers a vibrant atmosphere with numerous shops, cafes, and restaurants.

Highlights: Artus Court, Gdansk Shakespeare Theatre, and numerous shops along Piwna Street.

3. Gdansk Shipyard (Stocznia Gdańska):
This region played a pivotal role
in the history of Gdansk and Europe. It is where the Solidarity Movement, led by Lech Walesa, originated. The shipyard's historical significance is commemorated with monuments and museums.

Highlights: European Solidarity Centre, Monument to the Fallen Shipyard Workers, and Gdansk Shipyard Museum.

4. Oliwa:

Located in the northern part of Gdansk, Oliwa is known for its peaceful ambiance and green spaces. It's a district that offers a relaxing escape from the city's hustle and bustle.

Highlights: Oliwa Park, Oliwa Cathedral with its famous organ, and the picturesque Oliwa Zoo.

5. Wrzeszcz:

Wrzeszcz is a dynamic district known for its lively atmosphere, shopping streets, and a

mix of historic and modern architecture. It's home to Gdansk's main railway station.
Highlights: Galeria Bałtycka shopping mall, Körner Park, and the iconic Wrzeszcz Railway Station.

6. Gdańsk Oświęcim Estate (Osiedle Gdańsk Oświęcim)

This residential neighborhood offers a glimpse into everyday life in Gdansk. It's a quieter area with parks and local shops.
Highlights: Park Oliwski, local cafes, and the laid-back atmosphere.

7. Przymorze:

Przymorze is located near the Baltic Sea and is known for its coastal areas and modern apartment buildings. It's a popular destination for beachgoers and outdoor enthusiasts.
Highlights: Jelitkowo Beach, Ronald Reagan Park, and the nearby Brzeźno Beach.

8. Górny Sopot:

Górny Sopot is part of the neighboring city of Sopot but is easily accessible from Gdansk. It's famous for its spa culture, historic wooden architecture, and the iconic Sopot Pier.

Highlights: Sopot Pier, Monte Cassino Street, and the Sopot Lighthouse.

Each of these regions in Gdansk offers a unique experience, from the historical treasures of the Old Town to the relaxing coastal areas of Przymorze and Górny Sopot. Exploring these regions will provide a well-rounded perspective of Gdansk's diverse offerings during your 2024 adventure.

3

Getting to Gdansk

Arriving by Train

If you plan to arrive in Gdansk by train during your 2024 adventure, you'll find that the city's main railway station, Gdańsk Główny, is a well-connected transportation hub with modern amenities. Here's what you need to know about arriving by train in Gdansk:

1. Gdańsk Główny Railway Station:

Location: Gdańsk Główny is centrally located in the Main City district, making it convenient for travelers to access the city's attractions and accommodations.

Modern Facilities: The station underwent significant renovations in recent years, resulting in a modern and passenger-friendly facility with shops, cafes, waiting areas, and information desks.

Ticketing: You can purchase tickets at the station's ticket counters or use automated ticket machines. Be sure to check the train schedule and book your tickets in advance if possible, especially during peak travel seasons.

International Connections: Gdańsk Główny is well-connected to major Polish cities and international destinations, including trains to Warsaw, Krakow, and Berlin. It's a key transport hub for travelers exploring the region.

2. Timetable and Services:

Timetable: Trains to Gdansk run regularly, but schedules may vary depending on the route and the time of day. Check the latest timetable online or inquire at the station for up-to-date information.

Classes of Service: Trains in Poland offer different classes of service, including Express (Express), InterCity (IC), and regional trains (Przewozy Regionalne). The choice depends on your preferences and budget.

3. Transportation from the Station:

Public Transport: Gdańsk's efficient public transportation system includes trams and buses, making it easy to reach your final destination within the city from the train station. Ticket machines are available at the station.

Taxis: Taxis are readily available outside the station. Ensure that you choose a licensed taxi with a visible rate card.

4. Accommodations:

Hotels: You'll find a range of hotels and accommodations within walking distance or a short tram ride from Gdańsk Główny. Booking in advance is recommended, especially during peak tourist seasons.

5. Exploring Gdansk:

Old Town: Gdańsk's picturesque Old Town is within walking distance of the station. You can start exploring historic sites, museums, and restaurants as soon as you arrive.

Tourist Information: Look for the tourist information desk at the station for maps, brochures, and assistance with planning your stay.

6. Language: While English is spoken at the railway station, it's a good idea to have some basic Polish phrases or a translation app handy to enhance your communication.

Arriving in Gdansk by train offers a convenient and scenic way to begin your adventure in this historic city. Whether you're traveling from within Poland or internationally, Gdańsk Główny provides a welcoming gateway to the beauty and culture of Gdansk in 2024.

Arriving by Bus

If you're planning to arrive in Gdansk by bus during your 2024 adventure, you'll find that the city's central bus station, Gdańsk Główny Bus Station, is a key transportation hub with various amenities and excellent connections. Here's what you need to know about arriving by bus in Gdansk:

1. Gdańsk Główny Bus Station:

Location: The bus station is conveniently located in the Main City district, close to the Old Town and within easy reach of major attractions, accommodations, and public transportation.
Facilities: Gdańsk Główny Bus Station offers modern facilities, including waiting areas, ticket counters, luggage storage, restrooms, and shops.

Ticketing: You can purchase bus tickets at the station's ticket offices or use automated ticket machines. It's advisable to check bus schedules and book tickets in advance, especially during peak travel seasons.

2. Bus Services:

Domestic and International Connections: The bus station serves both domestic and international travelers, with connections to various Polish cities and European destinations.

Operators: Multiple bus companies operate from Gdańsk Główny Bus Station, offering a range of service levels, including standard, express, and luxury buses.

Timetable: Bus schedules may vary depending on the route and operator, so it's important to verify the timetable for your specific journey.

3. Transportation from the Station:

Public Transport: Gdańsk has an extensive public transportation network that includes trams and buses. You can easily access the city center and other neighborhoods from the bus station. Ticket machines are available for purchasing tram and bus tickets.

Taxis: Licensed taxis are typically available near the bus station for travelers who prefer a more convenient and direct mode of transport to their accommodations.

4. Accommodations:

Hotels: You'll find a variety of hotels, hostels, and guesthouses in close proximity to Gdańsk Główny Bus Station. Booking your accommodations in advance is recommended, particularly during peak tourist seasons.

5. Exploring Gdansk:

Old Town: Gdańsk's charming Old Town is just a short walk from the bus station. This historic area offers numerous attractions, restaurants, and shops for you to explore upon arrival.

Tourist Information: Seek assistance and gather information about the city from the tourist information desk located within the bus station.

6. Language: While English is widely spoken at the bus station, having some basic Polish phrases or a translation app can be helpful for smoother communication during your stay.

Arriving by bus at Gdańsk Główny Bus Station provides an accessible and efficient way to commence your adventure in this culturally rich city. Whether you're arriving from another Polish city or an international destination, the bus station serves as a gateway to the beauty and history of Gdansk in 2024.

Arriving by Car

Gdansk, a picturesque city located on the Baltic Sea coast of Poland, is a destination that attracts travelers from near and far. Whether you're a seasoned traveler or someone looking to explore this charming city for the first time, arriving by car can offer a unique and flexible way to experience Gdansk and its surrounding areas.

As a writer specializing in travel guides, you understand the importance of detailed information and helpful tips for travelers. Let's explore what you need to know when arriving by car in Gdansk.

1. Planning Your Route

Before embarking on your journey to Gdansk, it's crucial to plan your route carefully. Depending on your starting point, you may need to cross borders or travel through different regions of Poland. Ensure you have a reliable GPS or navigation app to guide you along the way.

2. Border Crossings

If you're arriving in Gdansk from another country, be prepared for border crossings. Poland is a member of the European Union, so travelers from EU countries generally experience smooth border crossings. However, it's essential to have your identification, vehicle registration, and insurance documents readily available for inspection.

3. Road Conditions

Poland has a well-maintained road network, but road conditions can vary. Major highways (autostrady) are usually in excellent shape, while rural roads may be narrower and less smooth. Pay attention to road signs, speed limits, and be cautious of any ongoing roadworks.

4. Parking in Gdansk

Parking in Gdansk's city center can be challenging, especially during peak tourist seasons. Look for designated parking lots or garages and consider using the Parkopedia app to find available parking spaces. Be prepared to pay for parking, and keep an eye on any time limits.

5. Environmental Zones

Some areas in Gdansk may be subject to environmental zones, which restrict access to certain vehicles to reduce pollution. Check in advance if your vehicle meets the requirements for entry into these zones.

6. Exploring Gdansk

Once you've safely arrived in Gdansk, you'll find that having a car can be advantageous for exploring the surrounding areas, including Sopot and Gdynia. However, the historic city center is best explored on foot due to narrow streets and limited parking.

7. Public Transportation

Consider using Gdansk's efficient public transportation system to navigate the city center. Trams and buses provide convenient options for getting around, allowing you to leave your car parked securely while you explore the city's historic sites and vibrant culture.

In conclusion, arriving in Gdansk by car can be a rewarding experience, offering the freedom to explore the city and its surroundings at your own pace. However, thorough planning, awareness of road conditions, and knowledge of parking options are essential for a smooth journey. Gdansk awaits with its rich history, stunning architecture, and captivating atmosphere, ready to be discovered by travelers like you, who are passionate about exploring and writing about the world's wonders.

Airport and Transportation Tips

As a writer specializing in travel guides, your expertise lies in providing valuable information to fellow travelers. Whether you're planning a trip to a new destination or helping others explore, airport and transportation tips are vital for a smooth and enjoyable journey. Let's delve into some essential advice in this regard.

Choosing the Right Airport

Selecting the most convenient airport for your destination is the first step in planning your trip. Consider factors like proximity to your final destination, available airlines, and flight schedules. In Gdansk, Poland, the primary airport serving the region is Gdansk Lech Walesa Airport (GDN). It's well-connected to various European cities, making it a convenient choice for travelers.

Booking Flights

When booking flights, flexibility can save you money. Use fare comparison websites and apps to find the best deals. Be open to different travel dates and times, as flights during off-peak hours or mid-week may be more affordable. Additionally, signing up for airline newsletters or loyalty programs can provide access to exclusive discounts and promotions.

Packing Smart

Packing efficiently can make your journey more comfortable. Check your airline's baggage policies to avoid unexpected fees. Pack essentials in your carry-on, including travel documents, medications, and a change of clothes in case of delays or lost luggage. Don't forget to pack a travel adapter if you're visiting a country with different electrical outlets.

Airport Security

Navigating airport security can be a breeze with a few precautions. Arrive at the airport well in advance to allow time for check-in and security checks. Ensure liquids and gels in your carry-on adhere to the airline's size restrictions and are placed in a clear, resealable bag. Wear slip-on shoes to speed up the security process.

Transportation from the Airport

Upon arriving at Gdansk Lech Walesa Airport, you'll have several transportation options to reach your accommodation. Taxis, private shuttles, and ride-sharing services are readily available. Alternatively, you can use public transportation, such as buses or trains, for a cost-effective option. Research the transportation choices in advance to determine the best fit for your needs and budget.

Local Transportation

Understanding the local transportation system is essential for exploring Gdansk and its surrounding areas. The city offers an efficient network of trams and buses, making it easy to get around. Consider purchasing a transport pass if you plan to use public transit frequently during your stay. Familiarize yourself with routes, schedules, and ticketing options to make your journeys hassle-free.

Safety Precautions

Prioritize safety during your travels. Keep your belongings secure, be cautious in crowded areas, and avoid displaying valuable items. It's advisable to have a copy of your travel documents, including your passport and travel insurance, stored electronically in case of loss or theft.

In conclusion, a successful trip begins with careful planning and attention to detail, especially when it comes to airport and transportation logistics. By choosing the right airport, booking wisely, packing efficiently, and staying informed about local transportation options, you can ensure a smooth and enjoyable travel experience. Gdansk, with its rich history and vibrant culture, awaits your exploration, and these tips will help you make the most of your visit.

4

Exploring the Old Town: A Journey Through Gdansk's Rich History

As a dedicated writer with a focus on travel guides, you undoubtedly appreciate the allure of historic destinations, and Gdansk's Old Town is a gem that beckons exploration. This charming area, situated along the picturesque Baltic Sea coast in Poland, is a testament to centuries of history, resilience, and cultural richness. Let's embark on a journey through Gdansk's Old Town, where every cobblestone street and historic building has a story to tell.

1. Begin at Dlugi Targ (Long Market)

Start your exploration at the heart of Gdansk's Old Town, Dlugi Targ. This bustling square is lined with colorful townhouses, each adorned with unique facades. As you wander along this historic marketplace, take in the lively atmosphere, visit quaint shops, and perhaps enjoy a cup of aromatic Polish coffee at one of the cafes.

2. The Iconic Neptune's Fountain

A short stroll from Dlugi Targ will lead you to the striking Neptune's Fountain, a symbol of Gdansk. This 17th-century sculpture stands tall and proud, overlooking the square. It's a popular spot for both tourists and locals, offering an excellent photo opportunity and a chance to immerse yourself in the city's maritime heritage.

3. Visit St. Mary's Church

Gdansk boasts an architectural masterpiece in St. Mary's Church, one of the largest brick churches in the world. Its Gothic beauty is awe-inspiring, both inside and out. As you step inside, the grandeur of the interior, including its magnificent organ and intricate stained glass windows, will leave you in awe. Don't forget to climb the tower for panoramic views of the Old Town.

4. Discover the Artus Court

The Artus Court, once the meeting place for merchants and dignitaries, is a splendid example of Renaissance architecture. The intricately decorated facade and opulent interior reflect the city's prosperity during the Golden Age. Explore its rich history and perhaps catch a guided tour to gain deeper insights into Gdansk's past.

5. Wander the Cobbled Streets
One of the joys of exploring the Old Town is getting lost in its labyrinthine network of narrow, cobblestone streets. As a writer, you'll appreciate the opportunity to meander aimlessly, discovering hidden courtyards, charming boutiques, and cozy restaurants serving traditional Polish cuisine.

6. Amber Museum
Gdansk is renowned for its amber, and the Amber Museum, located in a historic building, provides a fascinating glimpse into the world of this precious gemstone. Explore exhibitions on amber's history, its role in Gdansk's culture, and marvel at stunning amber artifacts.

7. Waterfront Views

Conclude your Old Town adventure by strolling along the picturesque waterfront of the Motlawa River. Here, you can admire the iconic medieval crane and the maritime essence of Gdansk. Consider taking a boat tour to gain a unique perspective of the city from the water.

In conclusion, exploring Gdansk's Old Town is like stepping back in time while immersing yourself in a vibrant and living historical masterpiece. Each corner you turn, each building you admire, and each story you uncover adds to the rich tapestry of Gdansk's past and present. As a writer, your visit to this captivating Old Town will undoubtedly provide you with ample inspiration and material for your travel guide, allowing others to share in the enchantment of this remarkable destination.

Exploring the Old Town: A Shopper's Delight

Gdansk's Old Town, steeped in history and adorned with architectural wonders, offers much more than just a glimpse into the past. It's also a haven for shoppers seeking unique souvenirs, handcrafted treasures, and a taste of Polish culture. As a writer with a penchant for travel guides, let's delve into the enchanting world of shopping in Gdansk's Old Town.

1. Amber Galore

Amber, often referred to as "Baltic gold," holds a special place in Gdansk's culture. In the Old Town, you'll find a plethora of shops dedicated to this precious gem. From delicate amber jewelry to intricately carved amber figurines, the choices are endless. When shopping for amber, be sure to visit reputable stores to ensure authenticity and quality.

2. Polish Pottery

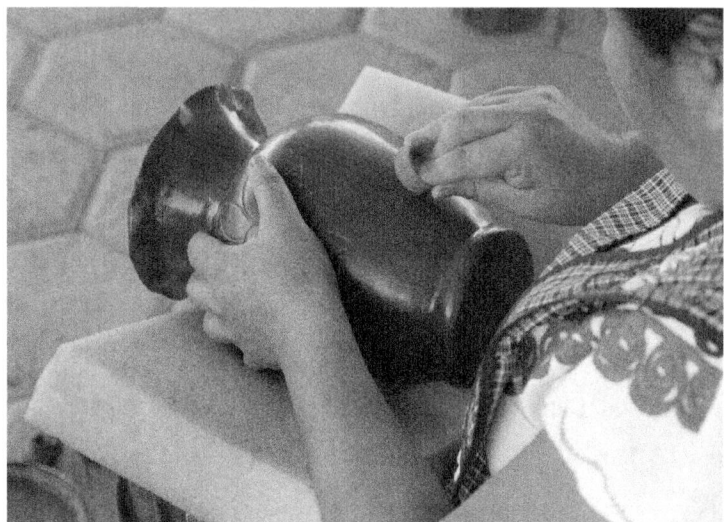

Gdansk is renowned for its stunning Polish pottery, known as "Boleslawiec." The colorful and hand-painted ceramics are not only functional but also works of art. Visit pottery shops to find a wide range of items, from plates and bowls to teapots and mugs. These pieces make for excellent souvenirs or additions to your own collection.

3. Handcrafted Goods

Artisans in Gdansk take pride in their craft, and you can discover a variety of handcrafted goods in the Old Town. Look for stores selling handmade leather goods, including belts, bags, and wallets. You'll also find locally made textiles, such as traditional Polish scarves and tablecloths, perfect for bringing a touch of Poland home with you.

4. Antique Treasures

For those with an appreciation for the past, antique shops in the Old Town offer a fascinating journey through time. Browse through vintage furniture, porcelain, artwork, and collectibles. Whether you're a serious collector or simply looking for a unique keepsake, you're sure to stumble upon hidden gems.

5. Traditional Polish Delicacies

Exploring the Old Town's market stalls and specialty food shops is a must for any food lover. Sample traditional Polish treats like pierogi (dumplings), kielbasa (sausages), and oscypek (smoked cheese). You can also find jars of pickled cucumbers, fruit preserves, and a variety of regional sweets to savor or bring home as gifts.

6. Art Galleries

Gdansk has a thriving arts scene, and the Old Town is dotted with art galleries showcasing the works of local artists. If you're interested in Polish contemporary art or want to bring home a piece of Gdansk's creative spirit, these galleries are the place to explore and perhaps make a unique purchase.

7. Souvenirs and Trinkets

Of course, no visit to the Old Town is complete without indulging in a bit of souvenir shopping. From Gdansk-themed T-shirts and postcards to wooden toys and folk art, there's a wide array of trinkets to remind you of your visit to this charming city.

In conclusion, shopping in Gdansk's Old Town is a delightful experience that allows you to not only collect mementos but also connect with the city's rich culture and heritage. As you explore the narrow streets and quaint shops, you'll discover a world of treasures waiting to be uncovered. Your travel guide writing expertise will undoubtedly find ample material in the Old Town's shopping scene, enriching the experiences of future travelers seeking the perfect Polish keepsake.

5

Gdansk's Historic Landmarks: A Tapestry of Time

Gdansk, a city that has weathered the storms of history and emerged as a vibrant jewel on Poland's Baltic coast, is a treasure trove of historic landmarks. As a writer whose craft revolves around travel guides, let's embark on a journey through Gdansk's rich history and explore the timeless beauty of its historic landmarks.

1. St. Mary's Church (Bazylika Mariacka)

Standing tall as a testament to Gothic architecture, St. Mary's Church is one of Gdansk's most iconic landmarks. Its towering spire, intricately adorned interior, and awe-inspiring stained glass windows make it a must-visit. Climbing the church tower rewards you with panoramic views of the Old Town.

2. Gdansk Crane (Żuraw Gdański)
The medieval Gdansk Crane is a symbol of the city's maritime heritage. This colossal wooden structure once played a crucial role in shipbuilding and trade. Today, it houses a Maritime Museum where you can learn about Gdansk's seafaring history.

3. Dlugi Targ (Long Market)
Dlugi Targ, the central square of Gdansk's Old Town, is a lively hub surrounded by colorful facades of historic buildings. The Neptune Fountain, Artus Court, and the Green Gate are just a few of the architectural wonders that grace this market square.

4. The Green Gate (Brama Zielona)
The Green Gate, an exquisite example of Northern Mannerist architecture, serves as the formal entrance to Gdansk's Royal

Route. Its elegant arcades and facade are a testament to the city's royal past.

5. Artus Court (Dwor Artusa)

Artus Court, a Renaissance-style gem, once hosted wealthy merchants and dignitaries. Its ornate interior and grandeur provide a glimpse into the city's Golden Age. Today, it houses a museum and is a cultural focal point.

6. Westerplatte

Westerplatte, a historic peninsula in Gdansk, is known for its significance in World War II. This is where the first shots of the war were fired. Visit the Westerplatte Monument and Museum to pay homage to the heroes who defended the post against overwhelming odds.

7. Oliwa Cathedral (Archikatedra Oliwska)

A short trip from the city center takes you to the Oliwa Cathedral, a masterpiece of Baroque architecture. Its breathtaking organ, adorned with intricate wood carvings and featuring over 7,000 pipes, is a highlight of the visit. Don't miss the charming Oliwa Park nearby.

8. European Solidarity Centre (Europejskie Centrum Solidarności)

A beacon of modern history, the European Solidarity Centre commemorates the Solidarity movement and its role in ending communism in Poland. The interactive exhibitions and the striking building itself make it a significant landmark.

9. Motlawa River Waterfront

The Motlawa River waterfront, with its historic warehouses and charming promenade, is a picturesque area to explore. You'll find delightful restaurants, cafes, and the opportunity to take boat tours along the river.

10. Golden Gate (Złota Brama)

The Golden Gate, a triumphal arch, marks the entrance to Gdansk's Old Town. Adorned with intricate sculptures and a clock, it's a magnificent symbol of the city's grandeur.

In conclusion, Gdansk's historic landmarks are like pages in a living history book, each narrating a chapter of the city's past. As a writer, your exploration of these sites will undoubtedly provide you with a wealth of material to craft a compelling travel guide, inviting others to embark on their own journeys through Gdansk's rich tapestry of time.

Sobieszewo Island and Beaches: A Coastal Paradise Unveiled

As a dedicated writer specializing in travel guides, you understand the allure of hidden gems, and Sobieszewo Island, tucked away on Poland's Baltic coast, is precisely that—a hidden paradise waiting to be discovered. Let's embark on a journey to explore the natural beauty and serene beaches of Sobieszewo Island, a destination that promises to captivate the hearts of travelers seeking tranquility by the sea.

1. Island Escape

Sobieszewo Island is a tranquil haven just a short drive from Gdansk's bustling city center. As you set foot on this pristine island, you'll immediately sense the slower pace of life and the soothing embrace of nature.

2. Pristine Beaches

The island's main draw is its pristine beaches. The long stretches of soft, golden sands invite you to relax, unwind, and bask in the coastal beauty. Whether you're a sunseeker or a beachcomber, Sobieszewo's beaches offer a serene escape.

3. Birdwatcher's Paradise

Sobieszewo Island is not only a retreat for humans but also a haven for birdlife. The island is home to the Sobieszewo Bird Reserve, a protected area where you can observe a variety of bird species, including migratory birds, making it a paradise for birdwatchers and nature enthusiasts.

4. The Dancing Forest

A unique natural wonder awaits on Sobieszewo Island—the "Dancing Forest" (Las Tańczący). Here, you'll find a grove of pine trees with twisted trunks and contorted shapes. The exact cause of this phenomenon remains a mystery, adding an air of intrigue to your visit.

5. Historic Fortifications

Explore the island's history through its well-preserved fortifications. The Fort of Sobieszewo, built in the 19th century, and the older Fort Wyspa are fascinating relics of a bygone era. You can take guided tours to delve deeper into the island's military past.

6. Tranquil Ambiance

Sobieszewo Island's charm lies in its unspoiled, laid-back atmosphere. It's an ideal place to escape the crowds and enjoy leisurely walks, bike rides, or simply savor the peace and quiet of the coastal landscape.

7. Local Flavors

After a day of exploration, indulge in the island's culinary delights. Seafood is a specialty here, and you can savor fresh catches at local restaurants. Don't miss the opportunity to try traditional Polish dishes with a coastal twist.

8. Accessible Adventure

Sobieszewo Island is easily accessible from Gdansk. A short drive over the bridge connects you to this coastal oasis. Consider renting a bicycle or taking a leisurely stroll to fully appreciate the island's natural beauty.

In conclusion, Sobieszewo Island is a coastal gem that beckons travelers seeking a retreat from the hustle and bustle of everyday life. Its pristine beaches, natural wonders, and tranquil ambiance create an inviting canvas for relaxation and exploration. As a writer, your visit to Sobieszewo Island will provide you with ample inspiration to weave its beauty and serenity into your travel guide, inviting others to discover this coastal paradise and experience the peace it offers by the sea.

Sopot and Gdynia Day Trips: Coastal Gems Beyond Gdansk

As a seasoned writer of travel guides, you appreciate the value of exploring neighboring destinations that enrich the overall travel experience. Sopot and Gdynia, two charming coastal towns nestled along the Baltic Sea, offer captivating day trip opportunities from Gdansk. Let's embark on a journey to discover the unique attractions and vibrant atmospheres of these neighboring gems.

Sopot: A Seaside Resort Extravaganza

Sopot, the "Riviera of the North," is a picturesque coastal town that seamlessly combines natural beauty with an inviting atmosphere.

1. Monte Cassino Street
Begin your Sopot day trip on the bustling Monte Cassino Street. Lined with cafes, restaurants, and boutiques, it's the perfect place for a leisurely stroll, people-watching, and indulging in local cuisine.

2. Sopot Pier (Molo)
Sopot boasts the longest wooden pier in Europe, extending gracefully into the Baltic Sea. Take a relaxing walk along the pier, breathe in the sea breeze, and enjoy panoramic views of the coast.

3. Beach Bliss

Sopot's pristine sandy beach is a magnet for sunseekers. Unwind on the shores, take a dip in the refreshing sea, or rent a beach chair and umbrella for the ultimate relaxation.

4. The Crooked House (Krzywy Domek)

The Crooked House is a whimsical architectural marvel that seems to defy gravity with its undulating facade. It houses shops, cafes, and art galleries, making it a must-visit curiosity.

5. Sopot Lighthouse

Visit the Sopot Lighthouse, an elegant structure with a rich maritime history. Climb to the top for breathtaking views of Sopot and the Baltic coast.

Gdynia: A Port City with a Maritime Soul

Gdynia, with its bustling port and maritime heritage, offers a unique blend of history and modernity.

1. Kosciuszko Square

Start your Gdynia exploration at Kosciuszko Square, a vibrant hub surrounded by cafes and shops. The monumental Gdynia Naval Museum is a prominent landmark here.

2. Gdynia Aquarium (Akwarium Gdynskie)

Delve into the underwater world at the Gdynia Aquarium. It features a diverse range of marine life, making it an educational and entertaining stop for all ages.

3. Gdynia's Modernist Architecture

Gdynia is known for its modernist architecture, characterized by functional and geometric designs. Take a self-guided architectural tour to admire these distinctive buildings.

4. Orlowo Cliff (Klif Orlowo)

For a touch of nature, head to Orlowo Cliff, a picturesque spot with scenic views of the Baltic Sea and stunning coastal cliffs. It's a peaceful escape from the city's hustle and bustle.

5. Emigration Museum (Muzeum Emigracji)

Explore the stories of Polish emigrants and their journeys at the Emigration Museum. The exhibits provide a deep understanding of Poland's diaspora.

6. Dar Pomorza Tall Ship

Marvel at the majestic Dar Pomorza tall ship, a floating museum that showcases Poland's maritime history. Climb aboard to experience life on a historic vessel.

In conclusion, day trips to Sopot and Gdynia offer a delightful contrast to the historical charm of Gdansk. Sopot's seaside elegance and vibrant street life create a perfect coastal escape, while Gdynia's maritime heritage and modernist architecture add a dynamic twist to your exploration. As a travel guide writer, your experiences in these neighboring towns will undoubtedly enrich your storytelling, allowing you to share the coastal allure of Sopot and the maritime soul of Gdynia with fellow travelers seeking diverse experiences on Poland's Baltic coast.

6

Museums and Cultural Attractions in Gdansk: A Journey Through History and Art

As a writer who specializes in travel guides, you understand the importance of immersing yourself in a destination's culture and history. Gdansk, with its rich heritage and vibrant arts scene, offers a treasure trove of museums and cultural attractions to explore. Let's embark on a journey through Gdansk's cultural tapestry and discover the museums and attractions that make this city a compelling destination.

1. National Maritime Museum (Narodowe Muzeum Morskie)

Begin your cultural exploration at the National Maritime Museum, a treasure trove of maritime history. Housed in a historic granary, this museum showcases ship models, maritime artifacts, and a captivating exhibition on the Amber Room's history.

2. Museum of the Second World War (Muzeum II Wojny Światowej)

Delve into the complexities of World War II at the Museum of the Second World War. Through immersive exhibitions, multimedia presentations, and artifacts, this museum offers a comprehensive understanding of the war's impact on Poland and the world.

3. European Solidarity Centre (Europejskie Centrum Solidarności)
Explore the spirit of resilience and change at the European Solidarity Centre. This interactive museum chronicles the Solidarity movement and its pivotal role in Poland's transition to democracy, making it a poignant cultural attraction.

4. Gdansk History Museum (Muzeum Historyczne Gdańska)
Discover Gdansk's history at the Gdansk History Museum, housed in the grand medieval Gdansk Crane. The museum offers insights into the city's past through exhibitions on trade, art, and daily life.

5. Gdansk Archaeological Museum (Muzeum Archeologiczne w Gdańsku)

For history enthusiasts, the Gdansk Archaeological Museum provides a deep dive into the city's ancient past. Explore archaeological finds, including artifacts from the medieval and Viking eras.

6. Polish Post Office Museum (Muzeum Poczty Polskiej)

Visit the Polish Post Office Museum to learn about the brave resistance efforts of postal workers during World War II. This museum commemorates their struggle against German forces.

7. Gdansk Art Gallery (Galeria Sztuki Współczesnej)

Experience contemporary art at the Gdansk Art Gallery, which features works by Polish and international artists. The gallery's exhibitions offer a fresh perspective on the city's artistic scene.

8. Shakespeare Theatre (Teatr Szekspirowski)

Catch a performance at the Shakespeare Theatre, a modern architectural marvel that pays homage to the city's historical ties to the famous playwright. The theater hosts a range of cultural events and performances.

9. Gdansk Philharmonic (Filharmonia Bałtycka)

Immerse yourself in classical music at the Gdansk Philharmonic. Attend a concert and appreciate the harmonious blend of culture and artistry in a stunning architectural setting.

10. Artistic Street Murals

Stroll through the streets of Gdansk to discover an array of artistic street murals. These vibrant creations adorn the city's buildings, adding a contemporary touch to its cultural landscape.

In conclusion, Gdansk's museums and cultural attractions offer a captivating journey through history, art, and the spirit of resilience. Your exploration of these cultural gems will undoubtedly provide you with a wealth of material for your travel guide, enabling you to share the vibrant cultural tapestry of Gdansk with fellow travelers eager to immerse themselves in the city's heritage and artistic expressions.

Gdansk Science and Technology Centre: A Journey into Discovery

As a writer dedicated to travel guides, you understand the importance of uncovering not only a destination's history and culture but also its contributions to science and technology. The Gdansk Science and Technology Centre is a gem that allows you to delve into the world of innovation and exploration. Let's embark on a journey to discover the wonders of this center and its significance in Gdansk's cultural and educational landscape.

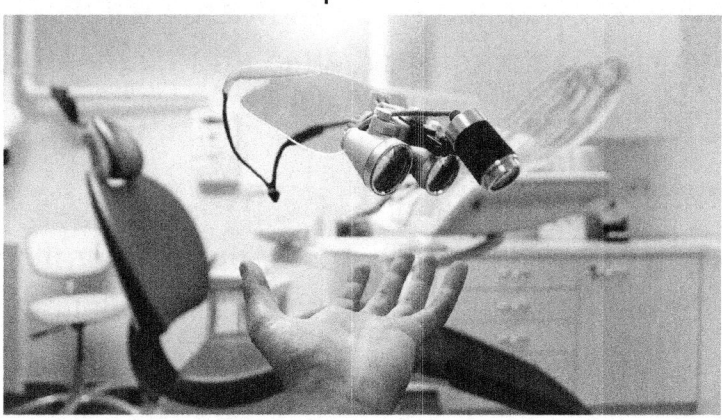

1. A Hub of Knowledge

The Gdansk Science and Technology Centre serves as a hub of knowledge and innovation, catering to both curious minds and aspiring scientists. As you step inside, you'll find a world of interactive exhibits, cutting-edge technology, and educational programs that make science accessible and engaging for all ages.

2. Hands-On Exhibits

One of the center's key features is its hands-on exhibits, designed to ignite curiosity and encourage exploration. Visitors can participate in various interactive displays, experiments, and demonstrations, making learning a dynamic and memorable experience.

3. Space Exploration

Delve into the realm of space exploration through captivating exhibits and simulations. Learn about celestial bodies, space missions, and the mysteries of the universe.

The center's space-themed displays offer a fascinating glimpse into the cosmos.

4. Robotics and Innovation

For those intrigued by robotics and technology, the Gdansk Science and Technology Centre showcases the latest advancements in these fields. You can witness robots in action, explore automation processes, and even try your hand at programming and robotics.

5. Educational Programs

The center's commitment to education extends beyond its exhibits. It offers a range of educational programs, workshops, and events that cater to students, educators, and the general public. These programs foster a love for science and technology and inspire future innovators.

6. Sustainability and the Environment

Gain insights into environmental sustainability and the importance of eco-friendly practices. The center's exhibits on renewable energy, climate change, and conservation highlight the significance of preserving our planet.

7. Inspiring Creativity
The Gdansk Science and Technology Centre also embraces the arts, demonstrating how creativity and technology can intersect. Explore the synergy between science and artistic expression through interactive displays and installations.

8. A Cultural Experience
Beyond its educational value, the center contributes to Gdansk's cultural landscape by fostering a sense of wonder and curiosity. It encourages visitors to appreciate the role of science and technology in shaping our world.

9. Inspiring the Next Generation

As a writer, you'll appreciate the importance of inspiring the next generation of scientists, engineers, and innovators. The Gdansk Science and Technology Centre plays a pivotal role in sparking young minds' interest in STEM (Science, Technology, Engineering, and Mathematics) fields.

In conclusion, the Gdansk Science and Technology Centre is a testament to the city's commitment to education, innovation, and the advancement of knowledge. Your exploration of this center will undoubtedly provide you with fascinating material for your travel guide, allowing you to share the excitement of discovery and the world of science and technology with fellow travelers eager to explore Gdansk's multifaceted cultural and educational offerings.

Gdansk Shakespeare Theatre: Where Art and History Converge

As a travel guide writer, you have a deep appreciation for cultural landmarks that transcend time and inspire creativity. The Gdansk Shakespeare Theatre, nestled in the heart of Gdansk, is a shining example of such a place. Let's embark on a journey to explore the rich history, artistic significance, and cultural tapestry that define this remarkable venue.

1. Architectural Splendor
The Gdansk Shakespeare Theatre is a true architectural gem, echoing the grandeur of

Elizabethan theaters. Its wooden structure, designed in the spirit of Shakespearean playhouses, transports visitors to a bygone era. The striking building stands as a testament to the enduring appeal of Shakespeare's works.

2. A Tribute to the Bard
This theater pays homage to William Shakespeare, one of the greatest playwrights in history. It's not just a place for performances but a living monument to Shakespeare's enduring influence on literature, drama, and the arts.

3. A Unique Theater Experience
Attending a performance at the Gdansk Shakespeare Theatre is a unique and immersive experience. The theater's design and acoustics create an intimate atmosphere that allows the audience to connect deeply with the actors and the timeless stories being told on stage.

4. Shakespearean Repertoire

The theater's repertoire primarily consists of Shakespearean plays, bringing the Bard's masterpieces to life in a way that honors their original spirit. Whether it's the tragedy of "Hamlet" or the comedy of "A Midsummer Night's Dream," these productions captivate audiences with their timeless themes.

5. Cultural Events and Festivals

Beyond Shakespearean plays, the theater hosts a variety of cultural events, including concerts, ballets, and literary readings. It's a dynamic cultural hub that contributes to Gdansk's vibrant arts scene.

6. Historical Significance

The Gdansk Shakespeare Theatre has a rich historical backdrop. It was built on the site of the original Shakespeare Theatre, which existed in Gdansk in the 17th century. The reconstruction of this theater in the 21st century is a testament to the city's dedication to preserving its cultural heritage.

7. Educational Initiatives

The theater also plays a role in education, offering workshops, lectures, and programs that engage with Shakespeare's works. It's a place where students, scholars, and enthusiasts can deepen their understanding of the Bard's literary contributions.

8. Contribution to Gdansk's Renaissance

The Gdansk Shakespeare Theatre is part of the city's cultural renaissance, contributing to its reputation as a hub of arts and culture. It aligns with Gdansk's commitment to fostering creativity and artistic expression.

In conclusion, the Gdansk Shakespeare Theatre is not merely a performance venue; it's a testament to the enduring legacy of William Shakespeare and a cultural beacon in the heart of Gdansk. Your exploration of this theater will undoubtedly provide you with rich material for your travel guide, allowing you to share the magic of this unique place with fellow travelers eager to immerse themselves in the world of Shakespearean drama and cultural history.

Wybrzeze Theatre: A Cultural Jewel of Gdansk

As a writer devoted to travel guides, you understand the significance of cultural landmarks that enrich a traveler's experience. The Wybrzeze Theatre in Gdansk stands as a testament to the city's vibrant arts scene and cultural heritage. Let's embark on a journey to explore the history, artistic significance, and the cultural tapestry that defines this remarkable venue.

1. A Cultural Legacy
The Wybrzeze Theatre is an integral part of Gdansk's cultural legacy. It has played a pivotal role in the city's artistic development and has been a stage for countless memorable performances over the years.

2. Architectural Beauty
The theater's architectural beauty is a sight to behold. Its facade, adorned with elegant

sculptures and classical design elements, is a testament to the city's commitment to the arts. The interior of the theater is equally stunning, with its opulent decor and comfortable seating.

3. A Varied Repertoire
The Wybrzeze Theatre offers a diverse repertoire that spans a wide range of genres, from classical dramas and contemporary plays to musicals and experimental performances. It caters to a broad audience, ensuring there's something for everyone to enjoy.

4. Contribution to Polish Theater
The theater has made significant contributions to Polish theater, nurturing talent and fostering creativity. It has been a launchpad for many renowned actors, directors, and playwrights, solidifying its place in the country's theatrical history.

5. Cultural Festivals

The Wybrzeze Theatre hosts cultural festivals and events that celebrate the arts. These gatherings showcase the rich cultural tapestry of Gdansk and provide opportunities for artists to share their talents with the community and visitors alike.

6. Educational Initiatives

The theater is not just a venue for performances but also an educational hub. It offers workshops, acting classes, and educational programs that engage with the community and nurture young talent, ensuring a vibrant future for the arts in Gdansk.

7. Community Engagement

The Wybrzeze Theatre actively engages with the local community, fostering a sense of unity and cultural appreciation. It provides a platform for dialogue, reflection, and artistic expression, making it a vital part of Gdansk's social fabric.

8. Historical Significance

The theater's historical significance is underscored by its endurance through various eras, including times of political and social change. It stands as a symbol of resilience, creativity, and the enduring power of the arts.

In conclusion, the Wybrzeze Theatre is not merely a performance venue; it's a cultural jewel that reflects Gdansk's commitment to the arts and its rich heritage. Your exploration of this theater will provide you with valuable material for your travel guide, allowing you to share the magic of this cultural hub with fellow travelers eager to immerse themselves in Gdansk's world of theater, artistry, and cultural vibrancy

Gdansk Philharmonic Hall: A Symphony of Culture and Elegance

As a writer dedicated to travel guides, you have a keen eye for cultural landmarks that elevate a traveler's experience. The Gdansk Philharmonic Hall, nestled in the heart of the city, is a true gem that resonates with the harmonious blend of music, culture, and architectural elegance. Let's embark on a journey to explore the rich history, artistic significance, and cultural tapestry that define this magnificent venue.

1. Architectural Grandeur

The Gdansk Philharmonic Hall is an architectural masterpiece that seamlessly blends classical and modern design elements. Its elegant facade and exquisite interior make it a visual delight. As you step inside, you'll be greeted by a sense of opulence and sophistication.

2. Acoustic Excellence

One of the hall's defining features is its exceptional acoustics. Designed to enhance the sound quality of performances, it offers an immersive auditory experience that elevates the impact of every note and melody.

3. A Hub of Cultural Excellence

The Philharmonic Hall serves as a hub of cultural excellence in Gdansk. It hosts a diverse range of performances, from classical symphonies and chamber music to contemporary concerts and cultural events. The venue's versatility ensures that there's something for every music enthusiast.

4. World-Class Performances

The hall has welcomed world-renowned musicians, conductors, and orchestras. Attending a performance here is not just an auditory delight but a chance to witness the brilliance of musical talents from around the world.

5. Education and Outreach

The Gdansk Philharmonic Hall is not limited to performances. It actively engages with the community through educational initiatives, workshops, and outreach programs. These efforts aim to nurture a love for music and ensure that it continues to enrich lives for generations to come.

6. A Cultural Landmark

The hall is a cultural landmark that symbolizes Gdansk's commitment to the arts. Its presence adds to the city's cultural vibrancy and underscores the importance of music in Polish culture.

7. Historical Significance

The Philharmonic Hall has a rich historical backdrop, having endured various chapters in Poland's history. It has witnessed moments of celebration, reflection, and artistic innovation, making it a significant part of the nation's cultural heritage.

8. Aesthetic Ambiance

The ambiance within the hall is carefully curated to enhance the concert experience. The combination of lighting, decor, and seating arrangements creates an inviting and immersive environment for music enthusiasts.

In conclusion, the Gdansk Philharmonic Hall is not just a concert venue; it's a sanctuary of culture, artistry, and architectural elegance. Your exploration of this hall will provide you with valuable material for your travel guide, allowing you to share the enchantment of this cultural treasure with fellow travelers eager to immerse themselves in Gdansk's world of music, refinement, and artistic splendor.

7

Gdansk's Cuisine: A Gastronomic Journey Through History and Flavor

As a dedicated writer of travel guides, I understand that a city's cuisine is a gateway to its culture and history. Gdansk, a city steeped in maritime heritage and regional traditions, offers a delectable tapestry of flavors that captivate the taste buds and tell a story of its past. Let's embark on a culinary journey through Gdansk's cuisine and discover the flavors that make this city a food lover's paradise.

1. Baltic Sea Treasures

Gdansk's location on the Baltic Sea provides a bounty of fresh seafood. Explore the city's fish markets and seafood restaurants to savor the catch of the day, including herring, cod, salmon, and smoked fish. Try "śledź w oleju" (herring in oil) for a taste of a traditional Polish delicacy.

2. Pierogi Paradise

Poland's beloved dumplings, pierogi, are a must-try in Gdansk. These pockets of dough can be filled with a variety of ingredients, such as mushrooms, meat, cheese, or potatoes. Top them with sour cream or butter for an authentic experience.

3. Polish Soups

Warm up with traditional Polish soups like "barszcz" (beetroot soup) or "żurek" (sour rye soup). These hearty and flavorful dishes are often served with sour cream and are a staple of Polish cuisine.

4. Kashubian Specialties

Gdansk is in close proximity to the Kashubian region, known for its unique cuisine. Don't miss the opportunity to taste "kartoflaki," potato pancakes served with various toppings, or "kaszëbskô mòwa," a hearty pork stew.

5. Street Food Delights

Exploring the streets of Gdansk offers a chance to savor local street food. Try "zapiekanka," a half-bagette topped with mushrooms, cheese, and other toppings, or "obwarzanek," a chewy pretzel-like snack.

6. Amber-Infused Treats

Gdansk is famous for its amber, and you can find amber-infused products in local cuisine. Try "likier bursztynowy," an amber liqueur, or amber honey, which pairs beautifully with cheese and bread.

7. Sweet Endings

Indulge your sweet tooth with Polish desserts like "makowiec" (poppy seed cake) or "pączki" (doughnuts). Visit local bakeries and cafes to sample these delightful treats, often accompanied by a cup of rich, aromatic coffee.

8. Craft Beer Revolution

Poland has experienced a craft beer revolution, and Gdansk is no exception. Explore the city's craft breweries to taste a wide range of innovative brews, from hoppy IPAs to rich stouts.

9. Mead and Traditional Drinks

Mead, known as "miód pitny," is a traditional Polish honey wine. Sip on this historic beverage, often served warm, to experience a taste of medieval Poland. Also, try "krupnik," a spiced honey liqueur.

10. Dining with a View

Many restaurants in Gdansk offer stunning views of the city's waterfront. Enjoy a meal while gazing out at the picturesque Motlawa River and the historic shipyards.

In conclusion, Gdansk's cuisine is a delightful fusion of maritime flavors, regional traditions, and Polish classics. Your exploration of these culinary treasures will provide you with a wealth of material for your travel guide, allowing you to share the gastronomic delights of Gdansk with fellow travelers eager to savor the city's rich history and diverse flavors.

Best Restaurants in Gdansk: A Culinary Odyssey

As a writer dedicated to travel guides, you understand that dining experiences can be a highlight of any journey. Gdansk, a city that blends maritime traditions with contemporary flair, boasts a vibrant culinary scene that caters to all tastes. Let's embark on a gastronomic journey through Gdansk's best restaurants, each offering a unique blend of flavors and ambiance that will leave a lasting impression on your readers.

1. Goldwasser Restaurant

Located in the heart of the Old Town, Goldwasser Restaurant is an elegant establishment known for its historic charm and fine dining. Indulge in Polish and European cuisine while enjoying views of the bustling Dlugi Targ. Don't miss the Goldwasser liqueur, a local specialty with real gold flakes.

2. Grand Cru Restaurant

For wine connoisseurs and food enthusiasts, Grand Cru Restaurant is a must-visit. This Michelin Guide-recommended restaurant offers a curated menu that pairs perfectly with an extensive wine list. The intimate setting and attentive service make it a memorable dining experience.

3. Pod Łososiem

As a writer with a penchant for seafood, Pod Łososiem is a seafood lover's paradise. This restaurant specializes in fresh fish and seafood dishes, prepared with a creative twist. The cozy interior and riverside location create a charming atmosphere for a seafood feast.

4. Restauracja Kubicki

Restauracja Kubicki is a culinary institution in Gdansk, known for its traditional Polish cuisine. Set in a historic building, it exudes an old-world charm. Try classic Polish dishes like pierogi, "bigos" (hunter's stew), and hearty meat platters.

5. Mamma Mia Trattoria

For lovers of Italian cuisine, Mamma Mia Trattoria offers a delightful escape to Italy. Savor authentic pizzas, pasta dishes, and fresh salads in a cozy, rustic setting. The welcoming atmosphere and friendly staff make it a favorite among locals and visitors alike.

6. Restauracja Mandu

Venture into the world of Asian flavors at Restauracja Mandu, specializing in Korean and Asian fusion cuisine. Sample delicious dumplings, bibimbap, and other Korean dishes in a modern and stylish setting.

7. Pierogarnia u Dzika
For a taste of Polish comfort food in a casual setting, Pierogarnia u Dzika is a top choice. This charming pierogi restaurant serves a variety of dumplings, both savory and sweet, making it an ideal spot for a quick and satisfying meal.

8. Gvara Restaurant
Gvara Restaurant offers a fusion of European and Polish cuisine with a focus on using locally sourced ingredients. The menu changes with the seasons, ensuring a fresh and innovative dining experience. The contemporary decor adds a touch of modern elegance to your meal.

9. Brovarnia Gdańsk
If you appreciate craft beer and hearty Polish dishes, Brovarnia Gdańsk is the

place to be. This brewery and restaurant offers a range of house-brewed beers to accompany traditional Polish cuisine in a historic and atmospheric setting.

10. Stary Dom Restaurant
Stary Dom Restaurant, located in a historic building, captures the essence of Gdansk's maritime heritage. Enjoy a selection of seafood dishes and Polish classics while surrounded by maritime decor and artifacts.

In conclusion, Gdansk's best restaurants offer a diverse range of culinary experiences, from traditional Polish fare to international flavors, all served in unique settings that enhance the dining experience. Your exploration of these culinary gems will undoubtedly provide you with rich material for your travel guide, allowing you to guide your readers through a culinary odyssey in Gdansk, where each restaurant promises a delightful journey of flavors and ambiance.

Local Markets and Street Food in Gdansk: A Feast for the Senses

As a dedicated writer of travel guides, you understand that exploring local markets and savoring street food is an essential part of immersing oneself in a city's culture. In Gdansk, a city with a rich maritime heritage and a vibrant culinary scene, you'll find a delightful array of markets and street food that cater to all tastes. Let's embark on a sensory journey through Gdansk's local markets and street food stalls, each offering a unique blend of flavors, aromas, and cultural experiences.

1. Hala Targowa Gdansk (Gdansk Market Hall)

Start your culinary adventure at Hala Targowa, the bustling market hall in the heart of the city. Here, you'll discover a treasure trove of fresh produce, meats, cheeses, and artisanal products. Engage with local vendors, sample regional specialties, and take in the vibrant atmosphere.

2. Gdynia Food Market (Targowisko Miejskie Gdynia)

For a taste of Gdynia's culinary offerings, visit the Gdynia Food Market. This outdoor market features a wide range of local and international foods, including fresh fruits, vegetables, seafood, and street food stalls. It's a great place to explore Gdynia's diverse flavors.

3. Gdansk Old Town Street Food

As you wander through the cobbled streets of Gdansk's Old Town, you'll encounter street food vendors offering a variety of local delights. Try "zapiekanka," a half-bagette with delicious toppings like mushrooms and cheese, or "oscypek," smoked cheese from the Tatra Mountains.

4. Obwarzanki

Obwarzanki are ring-shaped bread snacks similar to pretzels. Look out for street vendors selling these chewy delights throughout the city. They come in various flavors, from classic salted to sweet varieties like poppy seed.

5. Smak Piwa

At Smak Piwa, you can experience the burgeoning craft beer scene in Gdansk. This beer bar offers a wide selection of craft brews, often accompanied by food trucks serving up delectable street food to pair with your beer.

6. Herring Stalls

Gdansk's location on the Baltic Sea means you'll find an abundance of herring. Visit the herring stalls along the waterfront and sample different preparations, from pickled herring to creamy herring salads.

7. Food Truck Festivals

Keep an eye out for food truck festivals and events that frequently take place in Gdansk. These festivals bring together a diverse range of vendors offering everything from gourmet burgers and tacos to international cuisine.

8. Sopocki Bazar Smakoszy

Take a day trip to Sopot and explore the Sopocki Bazar Smakoszy, a food market where you can savor local and international flavors. It's an ideal place to indulge in street food while enjoying the coastal ambiance.

9. Traditional Polish Sausages

For a hearty street food experience, try traditional Polish sausages, known as "kiełbasa." Whether served on a roll with mustard or enjoyed on its own, it's a satisfying and flavorful option.

10. Amber-Infused Treats
Look for street vendors offering amber-infused products, such as amber honey or liqueurs. These sweet treats provide a unique taste of Gdansk's maritime heritage.

In conclusion, Gdansk's local markets and street food stalls offer a sensory feast that reflects the city's culinary diversity and cultural heritage. Your exploration of these vibrant food scenes will undoubtedly provide you with rich material for your travel guide, allowing you to guide your readers through an unforgettable culinary journey in Gdansk, where every bite tells a story of tradition, innovation, and the joy of savoring local flavors.

Craft Beer and Vodka in Gdansk: A Toast to Tradition and Innovation

As a writer dedicated to travel guides, you understand that a city's libations are a reflection of its culture and history. Gdansk, a city with a maritime heritage and a vibrant culinary scene, offers a diverse range of craft beer and vodka experiences that cater to all tastes. Let's embark on a journey through Gdansk's craft beer breweries and vodka traditions, each offering a unique blend of flavors, history, and cultural insights.

Craft Beer in Gdansk: Celebrating Innovation

Gdansk has witnessed a craft beer revolution in recent years, with breweries embracing innovation and quality to produce a wide range of beer styles. Here are some notable craft beer experiences in the city:

1. Browar Amber (Amber Brewery)
Browar Amber is a pioneering brewery in Gdansk, known for its commitment to craft beer excellence. Take a brewery tour to see the beer-making process firsthand and sample their diverse selection of brews, from hoppy IPAs to rich stouts.

2. Brovarnia Gdańsk
Brovarnia Gdańsk combines the art of brewing with a historic setting. Located in a 16th-century granary, this brewery offers a unique atmosphere for beer enthusiasts. Enjoy their house-brewed beers alongside traditional Polish cuisine.

3. Craft Beer Bars

Explore Gdansk's craft beer bars and pubs, where you can taste a variety of locally brewed beers. From small, cozy bars to lively establishments, these venues offer a chance to discover new flavors and meet fellow beer enthusiasts.

4. Beer Festivals

Keep an eye out for beer festivals and events that celebrate the craft beer scene in Gdansk. These gatherings often feature a wide range of local and international breweries, making it an ideal opportunity to sample a diverse selection of beers.

Vodka in Gdansk: Toasting to Tradition

Vodka holds a special place in Polish culture, and Gdansk is no exception. Here are some ways to explore the world of vodka in the city:

1. Vodka Tasting Tours
Embark on vodka tasting tours in Gdansk to learn about the history and craftsmanship behind this iconic spirit. Knowledgeable guides will introduce you to different vodka varieties and traditions while providing insights into Polish culture.

2. J. A. Baczewski Vodka Museum
Visit the J. A. Baczewski Vodka Museum to delve into the history of vodka production in Gdansk. Explore the exhibits, learn about the distillation process, and enjoy guided tastings of premium vodka.

3. Vodka Bars
Gdansk boasts numerous vodka bars where you can sample an array of vodka brands and flavors. Sip on traditional clear vodka or explore infused varieties with unique ingredients like herbs and fruits.

4. Traditional Vodka Rituals

Experience the traditional Polish vodka rituals, which often involve toasts and hearty appetizers. The practice of "na zdrowie" (cheers) is a central part of enjoying vodka with friends and locals.

5. Vodka and Food Pairings
Pair vodka with traditional Polish dishes for a complete culinary experience. Try vodka alongside pickled herring, smoked fish, or hearty sausages to discover the perfect flavor combinations.

In conclusion, Gdansk's craft beer breweries and vodka traditions offer a delightful blend of innovation and heritage, allowing you to toast to the city's maritime roots and culinary creativity. Your exploration of these libations will provide you with rich material for your travel guide, enabling you to guide your readers through a memorable journey of taste and culture in Gdansk, where every sip and toast tells a story of tradition, innovation, and the joy of raising a glass of life's moment.

8

Nightclubs and Bars

Gdansk, a picturesque city located on the Baltic coast of Poland, is known for its rich history, stunning architecture, and vibrant nightlife scene. While my primary expertise lies in travel writing, I can certainly delve into the realm of nightlife and guide you through the nightclubs and bars that add to the city's allure.

Gdansk's nightlife is a dynamic fusion of contemporary entertainment and the city's historical charm. Whether you're seeking a place to dance the night away or enjoy a quiet drink in a cozy setting, Gdansk has something to offer for every taste.

One of the most iconic nightclubs in Gdansk is "Parlament Club," known for its energetic atmosphere and live music events. Located in the heart of the Old Town, this venue attracts locals and tourists alike. The club's eclectic mix of music genres ensures that everyone finds something to groove to.

For those who appreciate a more laid-back ambiance, "Bunkier Club" provides a welcoming retreat. Nestled in a former bomb shelter, this bar offers a unique experience. The dimly lit interior, brick walls, and diverse drink menu create an intimate setting for conversation and relaxation.

If you're looking to combine your nightlife experience with a taste of local craft beer, "Brovarnia Gdansk" is the place to be. This microbrewery and restaurant offer a wide selection of freshly brewed beers and delicious Polish cuisine. It's a perfect spot to savor both the nightlife and the local flavors.

For a panoramic view of the city as you sip your cocktail, "Sky Bar" at the Radisson Blu Hotel is a top choice. Perched on the 27th floor, this upscale bar provides breathtaking vistas of Gdansk's skyline, making it an excellent location for a romantic evening or a celebratory night out.

Last but not least, "Prozak 2.0" is a renowned nightclub for those seeking an electrifying dance experience. With its cutting-edge sound system and a lineup of international DJs, it has earned a reputation as one of Gdansk's premier venues for electronic music enthusiasts.

In conclusion, Gdansk offers a diverse array of nightclubs and bars to cater to different preferences. Whether you're interested in dancing, live music, craft beer, or simply enjoying a quiet drink with a view, Gdansk's nightlife scene has it all. So, when you find yourself in this charming Polish city, be sure to explore its vibrant after-dark offerings, and you're bound to create unforgettable memories.

Live Music and Entertainment

Live music and entertainment hold a special place in the cultural tapestry of any city, and Gdansk, with its rich history and vibrant atmosphere, is no exception. In this essay, I will delve into the live music and entertainment options that grace this Polish gem.

Gdansk, nestled on the Baltic coast, has a thriving live music scene that caters to a wide range of tastes and preferences. The city's musical offerings span various genres, ensuring there's something for everyone.

For those seeking classical and orchestral performances, the Baltic Philharmonic is a true gem. Situated in an impressive modernist building, this renowned institution hosts symphony concerts, chamber music recitals, and opera performances. The acoustics are impeccable, and the grandeur of the venue adds to the overall experience.

If your musical taste leans more toward jazz, the "Zaklęte Rewiry" Jazz Club is a must-visit. This intimate venue is often hailed as Gdansk's jazz sanctuary, where talented local and international musicians take the stage. The dimly lit, cozy setting creates the perfect ambiance for a night of soulful jazz melodies.

For a blend of rock, pop, and indie music, "B90" is a hotspot. This multifunctional venue hosts concerts, art exhibitions, and cultural events. It's a favorite among the younger crowd, and the atmosphere is always buzzing with energy.

Gdansk also celebrates its maritime heritage with the "Shanties Festival." This annual event gathers musicians from around the world to perform sea shanties and maritime songs. The festival not only entertains but also pays homage to the city's seafaring traditions.

Moreover, Gdansk's vibrant street music scene adds an element of spontaneity to the city's entertainment landscape. While strolling through the Old Town's charming streets, it's not uncommon to encounter talented buskers playing traditional Polish tunes or contemporary melodies.

Beyond live music, Gdansk offers a variety of entertainment options. The city boasts a thriving theater scene, with venues like the Wybrzeże Theatre presenting a diverse repertoire of drama, comedy, and musicals.

Additionally, cultural events and festivals are frequently held throughout the year, celebrating everything from film and literature to food and art.

In conclusion, Gdansk's live music and entertainment scene is a testament to its cultural richness and diversity. Whether you're drawn to classical orchestras, jazz melodies, rock concerts, or the charm of street musicians, Gdansk has it all. It's a city where music and entertainment come together to create unforgettable experiences, enriching your visit and leaving you with a lasting appreciation for its cultural vibrancy.

Nighttime Strolls

In the heart of Gdansk, as the sun sets and the city's historic architecture begins to glow under the soft illumination of streetlights, nighttime strolls become a magical experience. These nocturnal wanderings allow you to immerse yourself in the city's rich history and ambiance in a way that daytime exploration cannot quite capture.

Begin your nighttime adventure in the Old Town, where cobblestone streets wind through a maze of beautifully preserved medieval and Renaissance buildings. The Main Town, or "Główne Miasto" in Polish, is particularly enchanting after dark. Its iconic facades, adorned with intricate architectural details, take on a fairytale-like quality when bathed in the warm glow of street lamps.

As you walk along the Royal Way, you'll pass by landmarks such as the Neptune Fountain and the Artus Court. These landmarks, when illuminated, evoke a sense of timeless elegance. The ambiance is tranquil, perfect for contemplative strolls or romantic moments.

Continuing your journey, cross the picturesque Green Gate, which separates the Main Town from the Motława River. The waterfront promenade comes alive at night, with restaurants and cafes offering al fresco dining. You can savor a meal while gazing at the reflections of centuries-old buildings in the shimmering waters of the river.

For a unique experience, consider visiting the medieval Gdansk Crane, or "Żuraw," which is beautifully lit at night. This historic structure is a symbol of Gdansk's maritime heritage and is a captivating sight against the night sky.

Beyond the Main Town, a stroll along Długi Targ Street is a delightful experience. This lively street is lined with colorful townhouses and inviting shops. Street performers often add to the festive atmosphere, serenading passersby with music or showcasing their talents.

If you're in the mood for a more contemplative walk, the St. Mary's Street, or "ulica Mariacka," is a hidden gem. Lined with amber shops and adorned with lanterns, this narrow, atmospheric street exudes a sense of intimacy. It's a serene place to explore, especially in the late evening when it's less crowded.

As your nighttime stroll continues, you may encounter unexpected delights, like the gentle melodies of street musicians or the captivating charm of street art. Gdansk's vibrant arts and culture scene often spills into the streets, adding to the city's allure after dark.

In conclusion, nighttime strolls in Gdansk are a journey through time and culture. The city's well-preserved historic architecture, combined with its contemporary vibrancy, creates an enchanting atmosphere that invites you to explore its streets and immerse yourself in its unique charm. Whether you're seeking romance, reflection, or simply the joy of discovery, Gdansk's nighttime strolls offer a memorable and magical experience.

Events and Festivals

Gdansk, a city steeped in history and culture, is not only a captivating destination for its architecture and scenic beauty but also a place where festivals and events bring its streets to life throughout the year. These gatherings celebrate the city's heritage, artistic prowess, and contemporary vibrancy, creating a tapestry of experiences for both residents and visitors.

One of Gdansk's most renowned festivals is the "St. Dominic's Fair" (Jarmark św. Dominika), which takes place annually in late July and early August. Dating back to 1260, it is one of the oldest trade and cultural fairs in Europe. The fair encompasses the entire Old Town, offering an array of goods, from crafts and antiques to regional foods and handmade products. Street performances, live music, and cultural events enrich the fair's atmosphere, making it a vibrant celebration of Gdansk's traditions and creativity.

For those interested in the maritime heritage of Gdansk, the "Hanse Sail Gdansk" is a must-attend event. Held in August, this festival gathers historical sailing ships from around the world along the Motława River. Visitors can explore these majestic vessels, watch maritime-themed performances, and indulge in delicious seafood dishes.

The "Gdansk Shakespeare Festival" is a cultural gem for literature and theater enthusiasts. Taking place annually in late July, it features performances of Shakespearean plays in various languages, as well as contemporary adaptations. The city's historic theaters, such as the Wybrzeże Theatre, become venues for these captivating performances.

Music aficionados will be delighted by the "Gdansk Music Festival" (Festiwal Muzyki Kameralnej), which usually takes place in August. This classical music festival showcases the talents of renowned international and local musicians in stunning historical settings, including churches and concert halls.

In addition to these annual events, Gdansk hosts a variety of cultural and artistic festivals that showcase contemporary creativity. The "Gdansk DocFilm Festival" celebrates documentary filmmaking, while the "Gdansk Dance Festival" features innovative and experimental dance performances.

To experience the magic of Christmas in Gdansk, the "Gdansk Christmas Market" is a must-visit. It transforms the city's squares into enchanting winter wonderlands, complete with festive decorations, artisanal crafts, and seasonal treats.

Moreover, Gdansk's calendar is often filled with smaller, niche events that cater to specific interests, such as the "Amberif" fair for amber enthusiasts or the "Gdansk Beer Festival" for craft beer lovers.

In conclusion, Gdansk's events and festivals are a testament to the city's dynamic cultural scene and its commitment to preserving its heritage while embracing contemporary creativity. Whether you're drawn to historic fairs, classical music, theater, or seasonal celebrations, Gdansk offers a diverse range of events that provide immersive experiences and create lasting memories. These gatherings not only showcase the city's cultural richness but also offer opportunities for visitors to engage with its vibrant community.

Nightlife Safety Tips

As you embark on your exploration of Gdansk's vibrant nightlife, it's important to prioritize safety to ensure a memorable and worry-free experience. Here are some essential safety tips to keep in mind while enjoying the city's nightlife:

Plan Ahead: Before heading out for the night, familiarize yourself with the layout of the city, the locations of the venues you plan to visit, and the best routes to get there. Having a plan can help you stay organized and avoid wandering into unfamiliar or potentially unsafe areas.

Stay in Well-Lit Areas: Stick to well-lit streets and popular nightlife districts, especially when walking from one venue to another. Avoid dark or deserted alleyways and shortcuts that may pose security risks.

Travel in Groups: Whenever possible, go out with a group of friends or fellow travelers. There is safety in numbers, and it's easier to watch out for each other. Make sure to establish a meeting point in case you get separated.

Keep Valuables Secure: Pickpocketing can happen in crowded nightlife areas. Keep your belongings, such as wallets, phones, and bags, secure and close to your body. Consider using a money belt or a crossbody bag with a secure closure.

Drink Responsibly: If you choose to consume alcohol, do so responsibly. Know your limits and pace yourself. Excessive drinking can impair your judgment and make you vulnerable to accidents or risky situations.

Use Licensed Transportation: When it's time to return to your accommodation, use licensed and reputable transportation options, such as registered taxis or rideshare services. Avoid accepting rides from unlicensed or unofficial operators.

Stay Hydrated: Alcohol can lead to dehydration, especially in crowded and warm venues. Drink water between alcoholic beverages to stay hydrated and reduce the risk of hangovers.

Trust Your Instincts: If a situation or person makes you feel uncomfortable or unsafe, trust your instincts and remove yourself from the situation. Don't be afraid to ask for help from venue staff or law enforcement if needed.

Know Emergency Numbers: Familiarize yourself with the local emergency numbers, such as the police and medical services, in case you need assistance. Keep your phone charged and easily accessible.

Designate a Driver or Arrange Transportation: If you're traveling by car, designate a sober driver or arrange alternative transportation in advance. Never drink and drive.

Be Mindful of Your Drinks: To prevent drink spiking, always keep an eye on your drink. If you set it down, don't leave it unattended. Consider using drink covers or lids.

Respect Local Laws and Customs: Be aware of and respect the local laws and customs in Gdansk. Different countries may have varying regulations regarding alcohol consumption, public behavior, and more.

By following these safety tips, you can ensure that your nighttime adventures in Gdansk are enjoyable and free from unnecessary risks. Prioritizing safety allows you to fully embrace the city's nightlife while maintaining your well-being and peace of mind.

Day Trips from Gdansk

Gdansk, situated in the heart of the Pomeranian region in Poland, offers an excellent base for day trips to explore the surrounding area. Here are some captivating destinations you can visit on day trips from Gdansk:

Sopot: Located just a short train ride away from Gdansk, Sopot is a charming seaside town known for its beautiful sandy beach, the longest wooden pier in Europe, and a lively promenade filled with restaurants, cafes, and shops. It's an ideal place for a relaxing day by the sea.

Gdynia: Another part of the Tri-City metropolitan area along with Gdansk and Sopot, Gdynia boasts a modern and vibrant atmosphere. Explore the city's maritime heritage at the Gdynia Aquarium and the

Dar Pomorza sailing ship, or simply enjoy the beaches and the Kosciuszko Square.

Malbork Castle: A UNESCO World Heritage Site, Malbork Castle is one of the largest brick castles in the world. It's an architectural marvel that offers insight into the medieval history of the Teutonic Knights. Trains from Gdansk can take you to Malbork in less than an hour.

Hel Peninsula: Known for its pristine beaches and natural beauty, the Hel Peninsula is a narrow strip of land between the Baltic Sea and the Puck Bay. It's a great destination for nature enthusiasts, and you can explore charming fishing villages along the way.

Kashubian Switzerland: The Kashubian region, known as "Kashubian Switzerland" due to its rolling hills and lakes, is a picturesque area for outdoor activities.

Hiking, cycling, and visiting charming villages like Kartuzy are popular options.

Westerplatte: Steeped in history, Westerplatte is where World War II began in Europe when German forces attacked a Polish military outpost. The Westerplatte Monument and Museum offer a somber but important glimpse into this historical event.

Hel: Located at the tip of the Hel Peninsula, this small town is known for its lighthouse, beautiful beaches, and the Hel Seal Sanctuary, where you can observe seals in their natural habitat.

Kashubian Ethnographic Park: This open-air museum in Wdzydze Kiszewskie showcases the heritage of the Kashubian people. You can explore traditional wooden buildings, learn about local crafts, and enjoy the serene surroundings.

Gdansk Bay: Consider taking a boat tour on Gdansk Bay to enjoy scenic views of the coastline and islands. Some tours even offer opportunities for fishing or birdwatching.

Tczew: A historic town located along the Vistula River, Tczew is known for its beautiful old town square and the impressive Tczew Bridge, a 19th-century engineering marvel.

These day trip options from Gdansk offer a diverse range of experiences, from exploring historical sites to enjoying the natural beauty of the Baltic Sea coast and its surrounding regions. Whether you're interested in culture, history, nature, or relaxation, there's something for every traveler within easy reach of Gdansk.

9

Currency and Banking

Understanding currency and banking in Gdansk, Poland, is essential for a smooth travel experience. Poland uses the Polish Złoty (PLN) as its official currency. Here's an overview of currency, banking, and money-related information you should be aware of while in Gdansk:

Currency Exchange:

Currency: The currency used in Poland is the Polish Złoty, abbreviated as PLN or zł. Banknotes come in various denominations, such as 10, 20, 50, 100, and 200 PLN, while coins are available in 1, 2, and 5 PLN denominations, as well as smaller denominations called grosz.

Exchange Rates: Exchange rates for foreign currencies can vary, so it's a good idea to check the current rates at a bank or currency exchange office (kantor) before exchanging money. Rates at airports or hotels may not be as favorable.

Currency Exchange Offices (Kantors): Kantors are widely available in Gdansk, especially in tourist areas and the city center. They offer currency exchange services, and many are open on weekends and holidays. While they generally provide competitive rates, it's advisable to compare rates at different kantors to get the best deal.

Banking and ATMs:

Banks: Gdansk has a well-developed banking system, and you'll find numerous banks and branches throughout the city. Some of the major Polish banks include

PKO Bank Polski, Pekao SA, and ING Bank Śląski.

ATMs: ATMs (Bankomaty) are widespread in Gdansk, and you can withdraw Polish Złoty using international credit and debit cards. Look for ATMs affiliated with major networks like Visa and MasterCard for wider acceptance. Most ATMs offer instructions in multiple languages.

Credit Cards: Major credit cards like Visa and MasterCard are widely accepted in hotels, restaurants, and shops in Gdansk. However, it's a good idea to carry some cash, especially for smaller purchases or in more rural areas where card acceptance may be limited.

Banking Hours: Bank opening hours in Poland are typically from 9:00 AM to 5:00 PM on weekdays, with some variations. Banks are usually closed on weekends and public holidays.

Currency Exchange at Banks: Banks also offer currency exchange services, but their rates may not always be as competitive as those at kantors. It's a convenient option if you need to exchange money during regular banking hours.

Safety Tips:

When using ATMs, be cautious of your surroundings and shield your PIN while entering it.

Keep your cash, credit cards, and important documents in a secure place, such as a money belt or a hotel safe.

It's a good practice to inform your bank about your travel plans to avoid any issues with card usage abroad.

Always have some local currency on hand for small expenses and places that may not accept cards.

In summary, Gdansk offers a well-established banking infrastructure, and you should have no trouble accessing cash or making card payments. Currency exchange offices and ATMs are readily available, making it convenient for travelers to manage their finances during their stay in this charming Polish city.

Communication and SIM Cards

Effective communication is essential when traveling, and in Gdansk, you'll find several options for staying connected through SIM cards and communication services. Here's a guide on how to manage communication and obtain a SIM card in Gdansk:

1. Mobile Network Providers:

Some of the major mobile network providers in Poland include Orange, T-Mobile, Plus, and Play. These providers offer a range of prepaid and postpaid SIM card options to suit your needs.

2. Purchasing a SIM Card:

SIM cards are readily available at various locations in Gdansk, including airports, convenience stores, mobile network provider shops, and kiosks. You can also purchase them online from the respective provider's website or at official stores.

3. Required Documents:

To purchase and activate a SIM card, you will typically need to provide a valid passport or other official identification. The process is straightforward and usually takes only a few minutes.

4. Prepaid vs. Postpaid:

Prepaid SIM cards are a popular choice for travelers. You can top up these cards with credit as needed and avoid long-term contracts. Postpaid plans require a contract and are more suitable for long-term residents.

5. Data Plans:

Most SIM cards in Poland come with data plans. Depending on your usage, you can choose from a variety of data packages. These packages usually include a certain amount of data, SMS, and call minutes.

6. Coverage:

Major mobile network providers have extensive coverage in Gdansk and throughout Poland. However, if you plan to visit more remote areas, it's a good idea to check coverage maps or ask locals for recommendations.

7. Wi-Fi Hotspots:

Gdansk offers free Wi-Fi in many public places, including parks, cafes, and some public transport areas. However, having a local SIM card ensures reliable connectivity wherever you go.

8. Communication Apps:

To save on international calling and messaging charges, consider using communication apps like WhatsApp, Skype, or Viber over Wi-Fi or mobile data.

9. Emergency Services:

The emergency number for police, fire, and medical assistance in Poland is 112.

10. Roaming:

If you plan to travel outside of Poland, check with your mobile provider regarding international roaming options and charges. Buying a local SIM card in each country you visit may be a cost-effective alternative.

By obtaining a local SIM card and following these tips, you'll be well-equipped to stay connected and communicate effectively while exploring the beautiful city of Gdansk and its surroundings. Whether you need to navigate the city, stay in touch with loved ones, or access travel information, reliable communication is essential for a memorable trip.

Internet and Wi-Fi Availability

Internet and Wi-Fi availability in Gdansk, Poland, is generally widespread, making it convenient for travelers to stay connected during their visit. Here's an overview of internet access options and where you can find Wi-Fi hotspots in the city:

1. Wi-Fi in Accommodations:

Most hotels, hostels, and guesthouses in Gdansk offer free Wi-Fi to their guests. The quality of Wi-Fi may vary, so it's a good idea to check with your accommodation about their internet services.
2. Public Wi-Fi Hotspots:

Gdansk provides free Wi-Fi in various public areas, including parks, squares, and public transport hubs. Look for signage indicating the availability of free Wi-Fi. These hotspots are often labeled as "Gdansk Free Wi-Fi."

3. Cafes and Restaurants:

Many cafes, restaurants, and bars in Gdansk provide complimentary Wi-Fi for patrons. You can enjoy a meal or a cup of coffee while staying connected.

4. Shopping Centers and Malls:

Large shopping centers like the Madison Shopping Gallery and the Forum Gdansk Mall typically offer free Wi-Fi to shoppers and visitors.

5. Museums and Cultural Institutions:

Some museums and cultural institutions in Gdansk offer Wi-Fi connectivity to enhance the visitor experience. Check with the specific venue for availability.

6. Libraries and Universities:

Local libraries and university campuses may offer public access to Wi-Fi. Check their policies for usage requirements.

7. Mobile Data and SIM Cards:

If you prefer a reliable and high-speed internet connection on the go, consider purchasing a local SIM card with a data plan from one of Poland's major mobile network providers. This allows you to have internet access wherever you travel within the country.

8. Internet Cafes:

While internet cafes have become less common due to the prevalence of smartphones and personal devices, you may still find a few in Gdansk if you require access to a computer and the internet.

9. Roaming:

If you're traveling from another European Union (EU) country, you can benefit from the "Roam Like at Home" policy, which allows you to use your home mobile plan's allowances (including data) in Poland without incurring additional roaming charges. Check with your mobile provider for details.

10. Co-Working Spaces:

Gdansk has a growing number of co-working spaces, which offer high-speed internet and a productive environment for remote work or business-related tasks. Some popular options include Creative Hub Gdansk and Pracownie Kreatywne.
In summary, Gdansk offers a variety of options for staying connected to the internet, from free public Wi-Fi to mobile data plans and co-working spaces. Whether you're a tourist looking to share your travel experiences or a business traveler in need of a reliable connection, you'll find that Gdansk has you covered in terms of internet and Wi-Fi availability.

Medical Services and Pharmacies

Access to medical services and pharmacies is essential information for travelers to Gdansk, Poland, to ensure their well-being during their stay. Here is a guide on medical services and pharmacies in Gdansk:

1. Hospitals and Medical Centers:

Gdansk has several hospitals and medical centers that provide emergency and non-emergency medical care to residents and visitors. Some of the notable medical facilities in Gdansk include:

Gdansk University Clinical Center (Uniwersyteckie Centrum Kliniczne w Gdańsku)

Independent Public Clinical Hospital No. 1 (Samodzielny Publiczny Szpital Kliniczny nr 1)

Pomeranian Center for Infectious Diseases (Pomorskie Centrum Chorób Zakaźnych)

2. Emergency Services:

In case of a medical emergency, dial the European emergency number 112. This number will connect you to emergency services for medical assistance, police, or fire.

3. Pharmacies (Apteka):

Pharmacies in Poland are known as "apteka." They are widely available throughout Gdansk, and you can easily identify them by the green cross sign. Most pharmacies in Gdansk are well-stocked and staffed by trained professionals.

4. Pharmacy Hours:

The operating hours of pharmacies in Gdansk may vary, but many are open during regular business hours, typically from 9:00 AM to 6:00 PM on weekdays and for a limited time on Saturdays. Some pharmacies in larger cities like Gdansk may offer extended hours or 24-hour services.

5. Prescription Medications:

If you have a prescription from a doctor, you can obtain your medications at a pharmacy in Gdansk. Make sure to bring your prescription with you.

6. Over-the-Counter Medications:

Pharmacies in Gdansk also carry a wide range of over-the-counter medications, including common pain relievers, cold and flu remedies, and first-aid supplies.

7. English-Speaking Staff:

In tourist areas and larger cities like Gdansk, you're likely to find pharmacy staff who can communicate in English. However, it can be helpful to have the names of medications or symptoms written down in case of language barriers.

8. Health Insurance:

If you have travel insurance or a European Health Insurance Card (EHIC), check the coverage details before seeking medical services in Poland. Keep copies of your insurance documents readily accessible in case you need medical assistance.

9. Traveler's Health Precautions:

Depending on your travel plans and health concerns, it's advisable to consult with your healthcare provider before your trip to ensure you have any necessary vaccinations or medications. This is especially important if you plan to explore rural areas or have specific health conditions.

10. COVID-19 Information:

Stay informed about the latest COVID-19 guidelines and restrictions in Gdansk, including mask mandates and testing requirements. Check with local authorities or your embassy for up-to-date information.

In conclusion, Gdansk offers access to medical services and pharmacies to cater to the healthcare needs of residents and tourists. While you're unlikely to encounter major health issues during your visit, it's always prudent to be prepared and have the necessary information on hand in case you require medical assistance or pharmacy services while exploring this beautiful Polish city.

Local Transportation

Efficient local transportation is crucial for exploring Gdansk and its surrounding areas. Gdansk offers a range of transportation options to help you navigate the city and its neighboring regions. Here's a comprehensive guide to local transportation in Gdansk:

Trams:

Gdansk has an extensive tram network that covers most parts of the city, including the Old Town. Trams are a convenient and affordable way to get around. They run frequently during the day and into the evening.

Buses:

Buses complement the tram system and serve areas not covered by trams. Gdansk's bus network is well-connected and reliable.

You can use trams and buses interchangeably with the same ticket.

Trolleybuses:

Trolleybuses are another mode of public transportation in Gdansk. They are electric buses powered by overhead wires. They primarily serve suburban areas and less central parts of the city.

SKM Trains:

The SKM (Szybka Kolej Miejska) commuter trains connect Gdansk with nearby cities like Sopot and Gdynia, forming the Tri-City metropolitan area. They are a quick and convenient way to travel between these cities.

Water Trams and Ferries:

Gdansk's proximity to the Baltic Sea means you can also use water trams and ferries to navigate the Tri-City area. These water vessels connect Gdansk with Sopot and Gdynia, providing scenic transportation options.

Taxi:

Taxis are readily available in Gdansk and can be hailed on the street or booked through ride-sharing apps. Make sure to use licensed taxis with visible meters and official markings.

Car Rentals:

While public transportation is convenient in Gdansk, some travelers may prefer to rent a car, especially if they plan to explore more remote areas or neighboring regions. Many car rental agencies operate in the city.

Cycling:

Gdansk is a bicycle-friendly city with dedicated bike lanes and rental stations (Bike Veturilo). Renting a bike can be an enjoyable way to explore the city, especially during the summer months.

Walking:

Gdansk's Old Town is compact and pedestrian-friendly, making it easy to explore on foot. Walking is a great way to immerse yourself in the city's historic charm and discover hidden gems.

Transportation Tickets:
You can purchase tickets for trams, buses, and trolleybuses at ticket machines, kiosks, or on board some vehicles. There are various ticket options, including single-ride tickets, daily passes, and monthly passes. Remember to validate your ticket before boarding.

Travel Cards:
Consider getting a Gdansk Tourist Card, which provides unlimited access to public transportation for a specific period and may include discounts on attractions. It's a convenient option for tourists.

Accessibility:
Gdansk is making efforts to improve accessibility for people with disabilities, with accessible tram stops, buses, and low-floor trams. However, it's advisable to check specific routes and stops for accessibility options.

In summary, Gdansk offers an efficient and diverse range of transportation options to suit different travel needs and preferences. Whether you're exploring the historic Old Town, traveling to nearby cities like Sopot and Gdynia, or venturing further afield, you'll find that Gdansk's transportation infrastructure makes it easy to get around and make the most of your visit.

Shopping in Gdansk

Shopping in Gdansk offers a delightful blend of traditional markets, modern shopping malls, and charming boutique stores. Here's a guide to the shopping scene in Gdansk:

Long Market (Długi Targ):

Located in the heart of Gdansk's Old Town, Long Market is a historic street lined with colorful townhouses and a vibrant market square. Here, you can find an array of souvenir shops, boutiques, and craft stores selling amber jewelry, traditional Polish pottery, and local artwork.

Mariacka Street:

This picturesque street, known as "ulica Mariacka," is famous for its amber shops. You can browse a wide selection of amber jewelry, including necklaces, earrings, and bracelets, often in unique and artistic designs.

Hala Targowa (Market Hall):

For a taste of local life, visit Hala Targowa, the city's main indoor market. It offers fresh produce, meats, baked goods, and local delicacies. It's an excellent place to sample regional foods and pick up ingredients for a picnic or to take home.

Madison Shopping Gallery:

Madison Shopping Gallery is a modern shopping center located near the Old Town. It houses a variety of international and Polish brands, making it a convenient option for fashion, accessories, and cosmetics.

Forum Gdansk Mall:

Another large shopping center, Forum Gdansk Mall, offers a mix of fashion retailers, electronics stores, and dining options. It's located in the Wrzeszcz district.

Stary Browar Gdansk:

While technically located in the neighboring city of Gdynia, Stary Browar Gdansk is a unique shopping complex housed in a historic brewery building. It features a blend of high-end boutiques, art galleries, and restaurants.

Gdynia Waterfront Promenade:

If you're interested in upscale shopping and dining with a sea view, consider taking a short trip to Gdynia's waterfront promenade, where you can explore boutiques, cafes, and enjoy the coastal ambiance.

Vintage and Antique Shops:

Gdansk has a growing vintage and antique scene. You can discover hidden gems and unique pieces in shops like "Stary Rynek" or "VINTAGE Bazar."

Local Food Markets:

In addition to Hala Targowa, you can explore local food markets, such as the Jarmark Dominikański, where you'll find fresh produce, dairy products, and artisanal goods.

Amber Museum Shop:
- The Amber Museum in Gdansk has a museum shop where you can purchase high-quality amber jewelry and unique amber-themed gifts.

Art Galleries:
Gdansk is home to several art galleries where you can purchase original paintings, sculptures, and other artworks by local artists.

Christmas Markets:
If you visit during the holiday season, don't miss the enchanting Christmas markets in

the Old Town. They offer handcrafted gifts, festive decorations, and seasonal treats.

When shopping in Gdansk, keep in mind that many stores may accept credit cards, but it's a good idea to carry some Polish Złoty (PLN) for small purchases or when shopping in smaller, cash-only establishments. Additionally, bargaining is not a common practice in Poland, so prices are typically fixed. Enjoy your shopping experience in Gdansk, where you can find a diverse range of items to suit every taste and interest.

CONCLUSION

In conclusion, Gdansk, with its rich history, stunning architecture, and vibrant culture, offers a captivating experience for travelers. Whether you're exploring the historic Old Town, enjoying the city's lively festivals, or embarking on day trips to nearby attractions, Gdansk has much to offer.

From the beautiful Long Market in the heart of the Old Town to the modern shopping malls and charming boutique stores, shopping enthusiasts can find a diverse array of items, including amber jewelry, traditional Polish pottery, and local artwork.

The city's transportation system, including trams, buses, and water trams, provides convenient ways to explore Gdansk and its surrounding areas. Whether you prefer public transportation or renting a bike to navigate the city's bike-friendly streets, you'll have no trouble getting around.

For those seeking medical services or pharmacies, Gdansk has a range of hospitals, clinics, and pharmacies, ensuring that your health and well-being are well taken care of during your visit.

Communication in Gdansk is made easy with accessible Wi-Fi, SIM card options, and reliable mobile networks. Staying connected while exploring the city and sharing your experiences with loved ones is hassle-free.

Nightlife in Gdansk comes alive with a variety of options, from live music and entertainment to nighttime strolls through the historic streets. The city's vibrant cultural scene, including festivals and events, provides an opportunity to immerse yourself in local traditions and creativity.

Finally, Gdansk's currency and banking services, including currency exchange offices (kantors) and ATMs, ensure that you have the necessary funds and financial services at your disposal.

In essence, Gdansk offers a rich and diverse experience for travelers, where history meets modernity, and where you can explore the past while enjoying the present. Whether you're a history buff, a shopping enthusiast, a culture seeker, or simply looking to relax by the Baltic Sea, Gdansk has something to offer every traveler. Enjoy your journey through this beautiful Polish city!

Share Your Thoughts on Our Gdansk Travel Guide!

Dear Valued Traveler,

We hope you had an incredible journey exploring the beautiful city of Gdansk, filled with rich history, vibrant culture, and unforgettable experiences. To continue improving and providing the best resources for future travelers, we kindly request your feedback on our Gdansk Travel Guide.

Your insights and opinions matter to us, and we would greatly appreciate it if you could take a few moments to share your thoughts. Your feedback will help us enhance our guide for others who embark on their own Gdansk adventures.

Please click on the following link to access the review form:
amazon.com/author/issacmarcos

Your input can cover various aspects of the guide, including the content, usability, and helpfulness. Whether you found the guide informative, user-friendly, or have suggestions for improvements, your feedback is invaluable to us.

As a token of our appreciation, all participants who complete the review will be entered into a drawing for a chance to win a [Prize Offer] as our way of saying thank you for your time and contribution.

Thank you for choosing our Gdansk Travel Guide, and we look forward to hearing about your experiences and insights. Your feedback will assist fellow travelers in making the most of their visit to this captivating city.

Warm regards and safe travels,
ISAAC MARCOS
isaacgbolahan7@gmail.com

Printed in Great Britain
by Amazon

28953827R00126